# The Science of Happiness

# The Science of Happiness: How to Cultivate Positive Emotions and Well-Being

## RIKROSES
## BOOKS AND E-BOOKS

# SUMMARY


**INTRODUCTION:** The Science of Happiness ...................................................................5

**CHAPTER 1:** What is Happiness and Why Does It Matter? ...........................8

**CHAPTER 2:** The Biological Basis of Happiness................................................10

**CHAPTER 3:** The Psychological Factors of Happiness....................................13

**CHAPTER 4:** The Social Aspects of Happiness....................................................15

**CHAPTER 5:** The Environmental Influences on Happiness..........................17

**CHAPTER 6:** The Spiritual Dimension of Happiness........................................20

**CHAPTER 7:** The Habits of Happy People ............................................................23

**CHAPTER 8:** The Practices of Happy People........................................................32

**CHAPTER 9:** The Skills of Happy People ...............................................................34

**CHAPTER 10:** The Strategies of Happy People ...................................................36

**CHAPTER 11:** The Challenges of Happiness .........................................................39

**CHAPTER 12:** The Paradoxes of Happiness ..........................................................42

**CHAPTER 13:** The Myths of Happiness ..................................................................44

**CHAPTER 14:** The Measurement of Happiness ...................................................47

**CHAPTER 15:** The Science of Happiness.................................................................50

**CHAPTER 16:** The Application of Happiness Science ........................................52

**CHAPTER 17:** The Promotion of Happiness Science.........................................59

**CHAPTER 18:** The Future of Happiness Science ................................................69

**CHAPTER 19:** The Personalization of Happiness Science...............................72

**CHAPTER 20:** The Reflection of Happiness Science.........................................78

**CONCLUSION:** The Science of Happiness .............................................................82

# INTRODUCTION: The Science of Happiness

Happiness is one of the most universal and elusive human pursuits. We all want to be happy, but what does it mean to be happy? How can we achieve happiness? And how can we sustain it in the face of life's challenges and uncertainties? These are some of the questions that the science of happiness seeks to answer.

The science of happiness is a multidisciplinary field that draws on insights from psychology, neuroscience, sociology, economics, philosophy, and spirituality. It explores the nature, causes, and consequences of happiness, as well as the ways to enhance it at the individual, interpersonal, and societal levels. It also examines the barriers, paradoxes, and myths that prevent us from being happy or make us unhappy.

This book is a comprehensive and accessible introduction to the science of happiness. It covers the main topics and findings of this fascinating and fast-growing field, as well as the practical implications and applications for our personal and professional lives. It also offers a personalized approach to happiness, helping you discover your own happiness profile and tailor your happiness practices accordingly.

In this book, you will learn:

- What is happiness and why does it matter for your health, well-being, and success?
- How does your brain produce and regulate happiness hormones and neurotransmitters?

- What are the psychological factors that influence your happiness, such as your personality, emotions, thoughts, beliefs, values, goals, and motivations?
- How do your relationships with others affect your happiness, such as your family, friends, colleagues, and community?
- How does your environment shape your happiness, such as your physical surroundings, culture, society, and politics?
- How can you connect with your spiritual side and find meaning and purpose in your life?
- What are the habits of happy people, such as gratitude, optimism, kindness, generosity, forgiveness, and compassion?
- What are the practices of happy people, such as meditation, mindfulness, yoga, exercise, sleep, nutrition, and hobbies?
- What are the skills of happy people, such as self-awareness, self-regulation, self-esteem, self-compassion, resilience, coping, and problem-solving?
- What are the strategies of happy people, such as setting goals, pursuing passions, finding flow, seeking challenges, embracing change, and overcoming obstacles?
- What are the challenges of happiness that you may encounter in your life journey, such as stress, anxiety, depression, trauma, loneliness, and grief?
- What are the paradoxes of happiness that may surprise or confuse you, such as the hedonic Treadmill, the adaptation effect, the happiness set point, and the Easterlin paradox?
- What are the myths of happiness that may mislead or deceive you, such as money buys Happiness, happiness is a destination, happiness is a constant state, and happiness is the same for everyone?
- How can you measure your happiness using various tools and methods, such as subjective well-being scales, happiness indices, happiness surveys, and happiness experiments?
- How can you apply the science of happiness to improve your personal and professional life, such as your self-care, your relationships, your work, your education, and your leisure?
- How can you promote the science of happiness to benefit others and society at large, such as your family, your friends, your colleagues, your community, and the world?
- What are the current trends and future directions of the science of happiness, such as positive psychology, neuroscience of happiness, happiness economics, happiness policy, and happiness technology?

- How can you personalize the science of happiness to suit your own needs and preferences, such as your happiness profile, your happiness style, your happiness strengths, and your Happiness challenges?

By reading this book, you will gain a deeper understanding of yourself and what makes you happy, as well as a broader perspective on the world and what makes it happy.

You will also acquire a set of tools and techniques that will help you enhance your own happiness and spread it to others.

This book is not a magic formula or a quick fix for happiness. It is a guide and a companion for your lifelong journey towards happiness.

Are you ready to embark on this journey?

If so, let's begin!

# CHAPTER 1: What is Happiness and Why Does It Matter?

Happiness is a word that we use often, but what does it really mean? How do we define it, measure it, and pursue it? And why should we care about it at all?

Happiness is a complex and multifaceted phenomenon that has been studied by philosophers, psychologists, neuroscientists, sociologists, economists, and many others. There is no single or universal definition of happiness, but rather different perspectives and approaches to understanding it. Some of these include:

- Happiness as a subjective state of mind or emotion, such as joy, satisfaction, or well-being.
- Happiness as an objective condition or outcome, such as health, wealth, or success.
- Happiness as a process or activity, such as living according to one's values, goals, or purpose.
- Happiness as a relationship or connection, such as love, friendship, or belonging.
- Happiness as a virtue or character trait, such as wisdom, kindness, or gratitude.

Each of these aspects of happiness can be important and valuable in their own right, but they are also interrelated and influenced by each other. For example, our emotions can affect our health, our goals can affect our satisfaction, our values can affect our actions, our relationships can affect our emotions, and our character can affect our relationships. Happiness is not a static or fixed state, but rather a dynamic and evolving one that depends on various factors and circumstances.

Happiness matters because it is an essential part of human nature and well-being. Happiness is not only desirable for its own sake, but also beneficial for many other aspects of our lives. Research has shown that happiness can:

- Enhance our physical and mental health, by boosting our immune system, reducing stress, and preventing disease.
- Improve our cognitive and creative abilities, by increasing our attention, memory, learning, and problem-solving skills.
- Strengthen our social and emotional skills, by fostering empathy, compassion, cooperation, and trust.
- Promote our personal and professional growth, by motivating us to pursue our passions, talents, and potentials.
- Contribute to our collective and global welfare, by inspiring us to act ethically, altruistically, and responsibly.

Happiness is not only a result of these benefits, but also a cause of them. Happiness can create a positive feedback loop that enhances our well-being and the well-being of others. Happiness is not a selfish or trivial pursuit, but rather a noble and meaningful one that can make the world a better place.

In this book, we will explore the science of happiness from various perspectives and disciplines. We will examine the biological basis of happiness in the brain and body; the psychological factors of happiness in the mind and personality; the social aspects of happiness in the family and community; the environmental influences on happiness in the culture and nature; the spiritual dimension of happiness in the faith and transcendence; the habits of happy people in their daily routines; the practices of happy people in their intentional activities; the skills of happy people in their coping strategies; the challenges of happiness in the face of adversity; the paradoxes of happiness in the contrast between expectations and reality; the myths of happiness in the common misconceptions and errors; the measurement of happiness in the scientific methods and tools; the application of happiness science in various domains and contexts; the promotion of happiness science in the public awareness and policy; the future of happiness science in the emerging trends and innovations; and the personalization of happiness science in the individual differences and preferences.

We hope that this book will provide you with valuable insights and practical tips on how to cultivate positive emotions and well-being in your life. We also hope that this book will inspire you to share your happiness with others and to contribute to the happiness of humanity.

9

# CHAPTER 2: The Biological Basis of Happiness

Happiness is not just a state of mind, but also a state of body. Happiness affects our heart rate, our body chemistry, and our physical health over time. In this chapter, we will explore the biological basis of happiness, and how our genes and hormones influence our well-being.

One of the first questions we might ask is: Are some people born happier than others? The answer is yes, to some extent. Every individual is born with a particular "happiness set point" or a baseline level of happiness, research suggests. After experiencing triumphs or tragedies, people adapt to their new circumstances and their emotions generally return to this genetically-determined level of well-being.

But how much of our happiness is determined by our genes? Studies based on European ancestry samples reveal that genetic differences between people account for approximately 40% of the differences in happiness, while the remaining variance is accounted for by environmental influences unique to an individual. This means that although we have a natural tendency to be more or less happy, we can also modify our happiness through our choices and actions.

One of the ways that genes influence happiness is through the production and regulation of neurotransmitters, which are chemical messengers that carry signals between brain cells. Some of the most important neurotransmitters for happiness are dopamine, serotonin, oxytocin, and endorphins. These chemicals are involved in various aspects of happiness, such as reward, motivation, pleasure, mood, social bonding, and pain relief.

10

Dopamine is often called the "reward" neurotransmitter, because it is released when we achieve a goal, receive positive feedback, or experience something novel or exciting. Dopamine motivates us to pursue rewarding activities and reinforces our learning and memory. Dopamine also plays a role in attention, creativity, and decision making.

Serotonin is often called the "mood" neurotransmitter, because it regulates our emotional state, especially our feelings of happiness and satisfaction. Serotonin also influences our appetite, sleep, memory, and social behavior. Serotonin levels are affected by various factors, such as sunlight exposure, diet, exercise, and stress.

Oxytocin is often called the "love" or "bonding" hormone, because it is released when we hug, kiss, or cuddle with someone we care about. Oxytocin promotes trust, empathy, and cooperation among people. Oxytocin also reduces stress and anxiety, and enhances our sense of well-being.

Endorphins are often called the "painkiller" or "runner's high" hormones, because they are released when we exercise, laugh, or experience pain. Endorphins act as natural analgesics that reduce our perception of pain and increase our tolerance for discomfort. Endorphins also boost our mood and energy levels.

As you can see, these neurotransmitters are essential for our happiness and well-being. However, they are not always in balance or in optimal levels. Sometimes, due to genetic variations or environmental factors, we may have too much or too little of these chemicals in our brain. This can lead to various problems, such as depression, anxiety, addiction, or aggression.

Fortunately, there are ways to enhance the production and function of these neurotransmitters naturally. Some of the most effective methods are:

Dopamine, serotonin, and oxytocin are neurotransmitters that play important roles in mood, motivation, reward, and social bonding. There are some natural ways to enhance the production and function of these chemicals in the brain, such as:

- Eating foods that contain amino acids, such as protein-rich foods, that are the building blocks of these neurotransmitters. For example, tyrosine and phenylalanine are precursors of dopamine, and tryptophan is a precursor of serotonin. Foods that are high in these amino acids include turkey, beef, eggs, dairy, soy, and legumes. Other foods that can boost dopamine levels

11

are bananas, almonds, avocados, and dark chocolate. Foods that can increase serotonin levels are oats, nuts, seeds, and salmon.

- Eating foods that contain probiotics, such as yogurt, kefir, sauerkraut, and kimchi. Probiotics are beneficial bacteria that can produce dopamine and serotonin in the gut and influence the brain through the gut-brain axis. Some studies have shown that probiotics can improve mood, cognition, and stress response in humans.

- Exercising regularly, especially aerobic exercise, such as running, cycling, swimming, or dancing. Exercise can stimulate the release of dopamine, serotonin, and endorphins, which are molecules that reduce pain and increase pleasure. Exercise can also improve blood flow to the brain and enhance neurogenesis, which is the formation of new brain cells.

- Getting enough sunlight exposure or using a light therapy device. Sunlight can boost serotonin levels by stimulating the pineal gland in the brain. Light therapy can also help people with seasonal affective disorder (SAD), a type of depression that occurs during winter months. Sunlight can also increase vitamin D levels in the body, which is essential for mood regulation and immune function.

- Practicing meditation, mindfulness, gratitude, or positive affirmations. These techniques can increase dopamine and serotonin levels by enhancing positive emotions and reducing stress. They can also help you develop a more optimistic outlook on life and cope better with challenges.

- Engaging in social activities that foster connection, trust, and intimacy. These can include spending time with friends and family, hugging, cuddling, kissing, or having sex. These behaviors can trigger the release of oxytocin, which is also known as the love hormone or the cuddle hormone. Oxytocin can also reduce anxiety, lower blood pressure, and promote healing.

These are some of the natural ways to enhance the production and function of dopamine, serotonin, and oxytocin neurotransmitters. However, if you are experiencing symptoms of low mood, anxiety, or depression that interfere with your daily functioning or quality of life, you should consult a doctor or a therapist for professional help. There may be other factors that affect your neurotransmitter levels or their receptors in the brain.

12

# CHAPTER 3: The Psychological Factors of Happiness

Happiness is not only a biological phenomenon, but also a psychological one. Our thoughts, feelings, beliefs, attitudes, and goals all influence our happiness levels. In this chapter, we will explore some of the psychological factors that contribute to happiness, such as:

- **Positive emotions:** How do positive emotions like joy, gratitude, love, and awe enhance our happiness and well-being? What are the benefits of experiencing and expressing positive emotions? How can we cultivate more positive emotions in our daily lives?

- **Positive thinking:** How do positive thinking styles like optimism, hope, and self-efficacy boost our happiness and resilience? What are the drawbacks of negative thinking styles like pessimism, cynicism, and self-doubt? How can we challenge and change our negative thoughts?

- **Positive self-concept:** How do positive self-concept components like self-esteem, self-compassion, and self-acceptance affect our happiness and satisfaction? What are the pitfalls of low self-esteem, self-criticism, and self-rejection? How can we develop a more positive and realistic self-concept?

- **Positive motivation:** How do positive motivation types like intrinsic motivation, autonomous motivation, and mastery motivation enhance our happiness and performance? What are the disadvantages of extrinsic motivation, controlled motivation, and performance motivation? How can we increase our positive motivation and reduce our negative motivation?

13

- **Positive goals:** How do positive goals characteristics like meaningfulness, specificity, and attainability increase our happiness and achievement? What are the challenges of pursuing goals that are meaningless, vague, or unrealistic? How can we set and pursue positive goals that align with our values and abilities?

- **Positive mindset:** How do positive mindset qualities like growth mindset, abundance mindset, and happiness mindset improve our happiness and potential? What are the limitations of fixed mindset, scarcity mindset, and unhappiness mindset? How can we adopt a more positive mindset that embraces change, opportunity, and happiness?

By understanding and applying these psychological factors of happiness, we can enhance our happiness and well-being in various domains of life. We can also overcome some of the common obstacles and barriers that prevent us from being happy. In the next chapter, we will examine the social aspects of happiness, such as how our relationships, communities, and cultures affect our happiness.

# CHAPTER 4: The Social Aspects of Happiness

Happiness is not only a personal experience, but also a social one. We are social animals, and we depend on others for our survival, well-being, and fulfillment. Our happiness is influenced by the quality and quantity of our social relationships, as well as by the social context in which we live.

One of the most robust findings in happiness research is that people who have strong and supportive social ties tend to be happier than those who are isolated or lonely. Social ties provide us with emotional support, practical help, companionship, and a sense of belonging. They also buffer us from stress, enhance our self-esteem, and promote our physical and mental health.

However, not all social relationships are equally beneficial for happiness. Some relationships may be toxic, abusive, or draining, and may undermine our happiness. Therefore, it is important to cultivate positive and meaningful relationships that enrich our lives and make us feel valued and appreciated.

One way to do that is to practice gratitude, appreciation, and kindness towards others. These positive emotions can strengthen our bonds, increase our trust, and foster mutual happiness. Another way is to engage in activities that bring us closer to others, such as sharing hobbies, interests, goals, or values. These activities can create a sense of commonality, cooperation, and community.

Another factor that affects our happiness is the social context in which we live. This includes the culture, norms, values, institutions, policies, and events that shape our society. The social context can influence our happiness by affecting our opportunities, resources, freedoms, rights, and responsibilities.

15

Some aspects of the social context that have been found to be related to happiness are:

- **Democracy**: People who live in democratic societies tend to be happier than those who live under authoritarian regimes. Democracy allows people to have a voice, a choice, and a say in their lives.

- **Equality**: People who live in more equal societies tend to be happier than those who live in more unequal ones. Equality reduces the gap between the rich and the poor, and fosters a sense of fairness, justice, and solidarity.

- **Trust**: People who live in more trusting societies tend to be happier than those who live in more distrustful ones. Trust enhances the quality of social interactions, reduces conflicts and corruption, and facilitates cooperation and collaboration.

- **Freedom**: People who live in more free societies tend to be happier than those who live in more restricted ones. Freedom allows people to pursue their own goals, values, and preferences, and express their true selves.

- **Peace**: People who live in more peaceful societies tend to be happier than those who live in more violent ones. Peace protects people from harm, fear, and trauma, and promotes security and stability.

In summary, happiness is not only an individual phenomenon, but also a collective one. Our happiness depends on the people we interact with and the society we live in. By enhancing our social relationships and improving our social context, we can increase our happiness and contribute to the happiness of others.

# CHAPTER 5: The Environmental Influences on Happiness

Our natural environment plays an important role in shaping our happiness. The quality of the air we breathe, the water we drink, the nature we enjoy, and the climate we live in can all affect our physical and mental well-being. In this chapter, we will explore how different aspects of the environmental quality influence our happiness, and what we can do to protect and improve our environment for ourselves and future generations.

One of the most obvious environmental factors that can impact our happiness is pollution. Pollution refers to the presence of harmful substances or contaminants in the environment that can cause adverse effects on human health and ecosystems. Pollution can come from various sources, such as industrial activities, transportation, agriculture, waste disposal, and household products. Some of the common types of pollution include air pollution, water pollution, soil pollution, noise pollution, and light pollution.

According to the World Health Organization (WHO), air pollution is one of the biggest environmental risks to health, causing an estimated 7 million premature deaths worldwide every year. Air pollution can cause or worsen respiratory and cardiovascular diseases, such as asthma, chronic obstructive pulmonary disease (COPD), stroke, and heart attack. Air pollution can also affect our cognitive abilities, mood, and happiness. For example, a study by Zhang et al. (2018) found that exposure to high levels of particulate matter (PM2.5), a common indicator of air pollution, reduced people's happiness levels in China. Another study by MacKerron and Mourato (2009) found that people reported lower levels of happiness when they were in areas with higher levels of nitrogen dioxide (NO2), another air pollutant.

Water pollution is another serious environmental problem that affects our happiness. Water pollution occurs when harmful substances or microorganisms contaminate water sources, such as rivers, lakes, oceans, and groundwater. Water pollution can result from agricultural runoff, industrial effluents, sewage disposal, oil spills, mining activities, and plastic waste. Water pollution can pose a threat to human health by causing diseases such as diarrhea, cholera, typhoid, hepatitis, and cancer. Water pollution can also damage aquatic ecosystems and biodiversity, reducing the availability and quality of fish and other food sources. Moreover, water pollution can reduce the aesthetic and recreational value of water bodies, affecting our enjoyment of nature and outdoor activities.

Soil pollution is another type of environmental degradation that can harm our happiness. Soil pollution occurs when harmful substances or agents accumulate in the soil, altering its physical, chemical, and biological properties. Soil pollution can result from industrial activities, agricultural practices, waste disposal, mining operations, and military actions. Soil pollution can affect human health by contaminating crops and food products with toxic metals, pesticides, or pathogens. Soil pollution can also reduce soil fertility and productivity, affecting food security and livelihoods. Furthermore, soil pollution can affect the natural beauty and diversity of landscapes, diminishing our appreciation of nature.

Noise pollution is the term used to describe any unwanted or disturbing sound that affects the health and well-being of humans and other organisms. Noise pollution can cause various problems, such as hearing loss, stress, high blood pressure, sleep disturbances, and impaired learning. Noise pollution can also harm wildlife by interfering with their communication, navigation, feeding, and reproduction. Noise pollution can come from many sources, such as traffic, construction, industry, aircraft, ships, and sonar devices.

According to the National Geographic Society, noise pollution is an invisible danger that cannot be seen, but is present nonetheless, both on land and under the sea. Sound is measured in decibels (dB), and sounds that reach 85 dB or higher can damage a person's ears. Some common sources of noise pollution that exceed this threshold are power lawn mowers (90 dB), subway trains (90 to 115 dB), and loud rock concerts (110 to 120 dB). Noise pollution impacts millions of people on a daily basis, and can cause Noise Induced Hearing Loss (NIHL), which is the permanent loss of hearing due to exposure to loud noises.

Noise pollution also affects the health and well-being of wildlife. Studies have shown that loud noises can cause physiological and behavioral changes in animals, such as increased heart rate, reduced growth rate, lower reproductive success, and altered

18

migration patterns. Animals use sound for a variety of reasons, including to find food, attract mates, avoid predators, and navigate. Noise pollution makes it difficult for them to accomplish these tasks, which affects their ability to survive. For example, birds may sing louder or at different times to cope with noise pollution, which can reduce their energy levels and make them more vulnerable to predators.

Noise pollution is a serious environmental issue that affects the quality of life of humans and animals. There are many ways to reduce noise pollution, such as using quieter machines and vehicles, limiting the use of loud devices in residential areas, implementing noise regulations and standards, using sound insulation and barriers, planting trees and vegetation to absorb noise, wearing ear protection when exposed to loud noises, and raising awareness about the effects of noise pollution. By taking these measures, we can protect ourselves and our environment from the harmful impacts of noise pollution.

Light pollution is the presence of unwanted, inappropriate, or excessive artificial lighting that can have negative impacts on humans, wildlife, and the environment. Light pollution is caused by various sources of electric light, such as street lamps, cars, buildings, outdoor advertising, and fireworks. Light pollution can create a bright glow in the night sky, called sky glow, that makes it difficult to see stars and other celestial objects. According to the World Atlas of Night Sky Brightness, more than 80 percent of the world's population and 99 percent of Americans and Europeans live under sky glow. Light pollution can also disrupt the natural circadian rhythms of living organisms, which are influenced by the cycle of day and night. This can affect sleep quality, hormone levels, mood, metabolism, and immune system. Light pollution can also interfere with the behavior and survival of nocturnal animals, such as birds, bats, insects, and turtles, that rely on darkness or moonlight for navigation, communication, reproduction, and predation. Light pollution can also increase atmospheric pollution by increasing the demand for electricity, which is often generated by burning fossil fuels. Additionally, light pollution can reduce the natural polarization of the sky, which is used by some animals for orientation. Light pollution is a global issue that can be reduced by improving lighting fixtures, adjusting types of light sources, re-designing lighting plans, and creating dark sky reserves.

# CHAPTER 6: The Spiritual Dimension of Happiness

What is the role of spirituality in happiness? How can we cultivate a sense of meaning, purpose, and transcendence in our lives? How can we connect with something greater than ourselves and feel a part of a larger whole? These are some of the questions that this chapter will explore, drawing on the insights of happiness science and various spiritual traditions.

Spirituality is a broad and complex concept that can be defined in many ways. Some people may associate spirituality with religion, while others may see it as a personal or secular experience. Some people may view spirituality as a belief system, while others may regard it as a practice or a way of life. Some people may consider spirituality as a source of comfort and guidance, while others may perceive it as a challenge and a quest. Regardless of how we define or approach spirituality, it is clear that it has a significant impact on our happiness and well-being.

One of the ways that spirituality influences our happiness is by providing us with a sense of meaning and purpose. Meaning is the feeling that our lives have significance and value, that we have a reason to exist and to contribute to the world. Purpose is the feeling that we have a clear direction and goal in life, that we have a mission or a calling to fulfill. Both meaning and purpose can enhance our happiness by giving us a sense of coherence, motivation, and fulfillment. They can also help us cope with adversity, stress, and suffering by providing us with a larger perspective and a deeper understanding of our experiences.

Another way that spirituality affects our happiness is by fostering a sense of transcendence and connection. Transcendence is the feeling that we can go beyond our ordinary limits and boundaries, that we can access a higher or deeper reality than the one we normally perceive. Connection is the feeling that we are not isolated or separate from others, but rather part of a larger whole, whether it is humanity, nature, or the divine. Both transcendence and connection can enhance our happiness by expanding our awareness, enriching our experience, and increasing our compassion.

How can we cultivate these aspects of spirituality in our lives? There are many paths and practices that can help us develop a spiritual dimension of happiness. Some of them are:

- **Meditation:** Meditation is a practice of focusing our attention on a chosen object, such as our breath, a word, or an image, in order to calm our mind and cultivate awareness. Meditation can help us achieve a state of mindfulness, which is the ability to be fully present and attentive to the present moment, without judgment or distraction. Mindfulness can enhance our happiness by reducing stress, improving mood, and increasing satisfaction. Meditation can also help us access states of transcendence, such as bliss, peace, joy, or love, by opening our mind to deeper levels of consciousness.

- **Prayer:** Prayer is a practice of communicating with a higher power or a sacred entity, such as God, an angel, or a saint. Prayer can take many forms, such as praise, gratitude, confession, petition, or intercession. Prayer can help us express our emotions, seek guidance, receive support, or offer service. Prayer can also help us connect with something greater than ourselves and feel a sense of belonging and trust.

- **Contemplation:** Contemplation is a practice of reflecting on a spiritual topic or question, such as the meaning of life, the nature of God, or the origin of the universe. Contemplation can help us gain insight, wisdom, and understanding about ourselves and the world. Contemplation can also help us transcend our ordinary thoughts and access higher levels of intuition and inspiration.

- **Service:** Service is a practice of helping others in need, such as volunteering, donating, or mentoring. Service can help us develop empathy, generosity, and humility, which are vital for spiritual happiness.

- **Yoga:** Yoga is a practice of harmonizing the body, mind, and spirit through physical poses, breathing exercises, and meditation. Yoga can help us

21

improve our health, balance our emotions, and connect with our true self, which are beneficial for spiritual happiness.

- **Nature:** Nature is a practice of spending time in the natural world, such as hiking, gardening, or stargazing. Nature can help us appreciate the beauty, diversity, and interdependence of life, which are conducive for spiritual happiness.

- **Art:** Art is a practice of expressing ourselves creatively through various mediums, such as music, painting, or writing. Art can help us explore our feelings, discover our talents, and share our vision, which are supportive for spiritual happiness.

# CHAPTER 7: The Habits of Happy People

What are the habits of happy people? How do they differ from the habits of unhappy people? And how can we cultivate the habits that promote happiness in our lives?

In this chapter, we will explore the answers to these questions, based on the latest scientific research on happiness and well-being. We will examine the habits that happy people have in common, such as gratitude, optimism, kindness, mindfulness, and self-compassion. We will also look at the habits that happy people avoid, such as rumination, perfectionism, comparison, and self-criticism. We will learn how these habits affect our happiness levels, and how we can change them for the better.

We will also discover how habits are formed and maintained, and what are the best ways to create new habits that support our happiness. We will learn about the role of motivation, intention, cues, rewards, and repetition in habit formation. We will also learn about the challenges and obstacles that we may face when trying to change our habits, and how to overcome them.

Finally, we will discuss how to apply the science of happiness to our daily lives, and how to make happiness a habit. We will learn how to create a happiness plan that suits our personality, preferences, and goals. We will also learn how to monitor our progress and evaluate our results. We will see how by changing our habits, we can change our happiness.

By the end of this chapter, you will have a better understanding of the habits of happy people, and how to adopt them in your own life. You will also have a practical guide to creating and maintaining habits that enhance your happiness and well-being.

## What are the habits of happy people?

Happiness is a complex and subjective phenomenon that depends on many factors, such as genetics, personality, environment, and behavior. However, some habits can help boost our happiness levels by enhancing our physical, mental, and social well-being. According to happiness experts and researchers, some of the most common habits of happy people are:

- **Experiencing flow often.** Flow is a state of complete immersion and engagement in an activity that challenges our skills and abilities. It makes us lose track of time and self-consciousness, and feel a sense of mastery and enjoyment. Flow can be experienced in various domains, such as work, hobbies, sports, or arts. Studies have shown that flow is associated with higher levels of happiness, creativity, and productivity.

- **Cultivating gratitude.** Gratitude is the appreciation of what we have and what others do for us. It helps us focus on the positive aspects of our lives, rather than the negative ones. Gratitude can be expressed in different ways, such as writing a thank-you note, keeping a gratitude journal, or saying a prayer. Research has found that gratitude can increase happiness, life satisfaction, optimism, and resilience.

- **Connecting with others.** Humans are social animals who need meaningful and supportive relationships to thrive. Happy people tend to spend time with their family and friends regularly, and to participate in their communities. They also show compassion, kindness, and altruism towards others, which can enhance their own happiness as well as the happiness of those they help.

- **Taking care of their health.** Happiness and health are closely linked, as they influence each other in both directions. Happy people tend to have healthy habits that protect their physical and mental health, such as exercising regularly, eating well, sleeping enough, and avoiding harmful substances. They also cope with stress effectively and seek professional help when needed.

These are some of the habits that can make us happier, but they are not the only ones. Happiness is also influenced by our personal values, goals, passions, and preferences. Therefore, it is important to find out what works best for us individually and to pursue it with enthusiasm and perseverance.

24

**How do they differ from the habits of unhappy people?**

Happiness is a universal goal that most people pursue in their lives. But what makes some people happier than others? What are the habits that distinguish happy people from unhappy people? According to various sources of psychological research, here are some of the main differences:

- Happy people enjoy every moment of their life, while unhappy people wait for something to make them happy. Happy people are proactive and seek fulfillment in their activities, relationships and goals. They appreciate what they have and live in the present. Unhappy people are passive and expect happiness to come from external sources. They are dissatisfied with what they have and live in the past or the future.

- Happy people are grateful for what they have, while unhappy people envy the success of others. Happy people acknowledge their achievements and the good things in their world. They express gratitude to themselves and others. Unhappy people focus on the material possessions and accomplishments of others. They feel inferior and resentful. They complain about their lack of luck and opportunities.

- Happy people are optimistic and resilient, while unhappy people are pessimistic and fragile. Happy people have a positive outlook on life and see challenges as opportunities for growth. They cope well with stress and adversity. They bounce back from failures and setbacks. Unhappy people have a negative outlook on life and see problems as threats. They cope poorly with stress and hardship. They dwell on failures and mistakes.

- Happy people are open-minded and friendly, while unhappy people are closed-minded and isolated. Happy people are curious and interested in learning new things and meeting new people. They are tolerant and respectful of different opinions and perspectives. They have strong social connections and support networks. Unhappy people are indifferent and fearful of change and diversity. They are intolerant and judgmental of those who disagree with them. They have weak or no social ties and feel lonely.

- Happy people are healthy and active, while unhappy people are unhealthy and sedentary. Happy people take care of their physical and mental health. They eat well, sleep well, exercise regularly, meditate, relax, etc. They have

25

high energy levels and good immune system functioning. Unhappy people neglect their physical and mental health. They eat poorly, sleep poorly, avoid physical activity, stress out, etc. They have low energy levels and poor immune system functioning.

These are some of the habits that differentiate happy people from unhappy people. Of course, happiness is not a fixed state that can be achieved once and for all. It is a dynamic process that requires constant effort and adaptation. Happiness is also influenced by genetic factors, personality traits, life circumstances, etc. However, by adopting some of the habits of happy people, we can increase our chances of experiencing more positive emotions and satisfaction in life.

**How can we cultivate the habits that promote happiness in our lives?**

Happiness is a desirable and elusive state of mind that many people strive for. But how can we cultivate the habits that promote happiness in our lives? According to psychology research, there are some strategies that can help us increase our happiness levels and well-being. Here are some of them:

- **Savor the moment.** Happiness is not only about achieving big goals, but also about enjoying the small pleasures of life. By paying attention to the present moment and appreciating what we have, we can enhance our positive emotions and reduce stress. For example, we can savor the taste of our favorite food, the beauty of nature, or the warmth of a hug.

- **Practice non-judgmental awareness of ourselves and others.** Happiness is not about being perfect, but about accepting ourselves and others as they are. By being mindful and compassionate, we can avoid harsh criticism and unrealistic expectations that can lower our self-esteem and damage our relationships. For example, we can remind ourselves that everyone has strengths and weaknesses, and that we are all doing our best with the resources we have.

- **Cultivate realistic thinking.** Happiness is not about denying or ignoring the negative aspects of life, but about facing them with optimism and resilience. By being balanced and rational in our thinking, we can avoid cognitive distortions that can amplify our problems and generate anxiety. For example, we can challenge our negative thoughts with evidence, consider alternative explanations, and focus on solutions rather than obstacles.

- **Connect with others.** Happiness is not about being isolated, but about being part of a supportive community. By building quality relationships with people who care about us, we can satisfy our need for belonging and receive emotional support in times of stress. For example, we can express our feelings and needs to others, listen empathically to their perspectives, and share gratitude and love.

- **Resolve conflicts proactively.** Happiness is not about avoiding or suppressing conflicts, but about resolving them constructively. By using assertiveness skills, we can communicate our opinions and preferences respectfully, without being passive or aggressive. For example, we can use "I" statements to express our feelings and needs, respect the other person's point of view, and look for win-win solutions.

- **Develop good self-care practices.** Happiness is not about neglecting ourselves, but about taking care of our physical and mental health. By engaging in healthy behaviors, we can improve our mood, energy, and immunity. For example, we can exercise regularly, eat nutritious food, get enough sleep, be kind to ourselves, and set healthy boundaries.

- **Share gratitude and love.** Happiness is not about taking things for granted, but about appreciating what we have and what others do for us. By expressing gratitude and love, we can strengthen our bonds with others, increase our positive emotions, and reduce our negative ones. For example, we can write a thank-you note to someone who helped us, give a compliment to someone who inspired us, or hug someone who comforted us.

- **Focus on the good.** Happiness is not about ignoring or minimizing the bad things that happen to us, but about acknowledging and amplifying the good things that happen to us. By focusing on the good, we can rewire our brains to be more positive and resilient. For example, we can write down three good things that happened each day, take pictures of happy moments, or keep a scrapbook of positive memories.

- **Live like you're on vacation.** Happiness is not about waiting for special occasions to have fun, but about creating opportunities to have fun in our everyday lives. By living like we're on vacation, we can increase our curiosity and enjoyment of life. For example, we can try new things, explore new places, or learn new skills.

27

- **Fake it until you make it.** Happiness is not only a result of our actions, but also a cause of them. By acting as if we are happy, we can trick our brains into feeling happier. For example, we can smile more often, use positive language, or adopt confident body language.

These are some of the habits that can promote happiness in our lives. Of course, happiness is not a one-size-fits-all concept; different people may find different strategies more or less effective for them. The key is to experiment with different habits and find out what works best for you.

Happiness is not a fixed state, but a skill that can be cultivated and practiced. One of the ways to increase our happiness is to adopt certain habits that happy people have in common. In this text, we will examine some of these habits, such as gratitude, optimism, kindness, mindfulness, and self-compassion. We will also look at the habits that happy people avoid, such as rumination, perfectionism, comparison, and self-criticism. We will learn how these habits affect our happiness levels, and how we can change them for the better.

Gratitude is the habit of appreciating what we have and expressing our thanks to others. Gratitude helps us focus on the positive aspects of our lives, rather than the negative ones. It also strengthens our relationships and makes us more generous and helpful. Studies have shown that gratitude can boost our happiness by up to 25%. To practice gratitude, we can keep a gratitude journal, write thank-you notes, or share our appreciation with others verbally.

Optimism is the habit of expecting good things to happen and seeing the bright side of situations. Optimism helps us cope with challenges and setbacks, and motivates us to pursue our goals. It also enhances our health and well-being by reducing stress and boosting our immune system. Studies have shown that optimism can increase our happiness by up to 35%. To practice optimism, we can reframe negative thoughts into positive ones, visualize positive outcomes, or use affirmations.

Kindness is the habit of being friendly, generous, and considerate to others. Kindness helps us connect with others and feel good about ourselves. It also creates a positive feedback loop, as kindness begets kindness. Studies have shown that kindness can improve our happiness by up to 20%. To practice kindness, we can perform random acts of kindness, volunteer for a cause, or compliment others.

Mindfulness is the habit of paying attention to the present moment with curiosity and openness. Mindfulness helps us savor the joys of life, reduce stress and anxiety, and regulate our emotions. It also enhances our creativity and productivity by improving our focus and memory. Studies have shown that mindfulness can increase our happiness by up to 15%. To practice mindfulness, we can meditate, do yoga, or engage in mindful activities such as walking or eating.

Self-compassion is the habit of treating ourselves with kindness and understanding when we face difficulties or make mistakes. Self-compassion helps us accept ourselves as we are, learn from our failures, and forgive ourselves. It also prevents us from being too harsh or critical of ourselves, which can lower our self-esteem and happiness. Studies have shown that self-compassion can boost our happiness by up to 10%. To practice self-compassion, we can use soothing words, gestures, or images when we feel bad, or write a letter to ourselves as if we were a friend.

On the other hand, there are some habits that happy people avoid, as they can undermine our happiness and well-being. These include rumination, perfectionism, comparison, and self-criticism.

Rumination is the habit of dwelling on negative thoughts or events from the past or the future. Rumination prevents us from enjoying the present moment, and amplifies our negative emotions. It also impairs our problem-solving skills and decision-making abilities. Studies have shown that rumination can decrease our happiness by up to 30%. To stop ruminating, we can distract ourselves with positive activities, challenge our negative thoughts with evidence or logic, or seek social support.

Perfectionism is the habit of setting unrealistic or unattainable standards for ourselves or others. Perfectionism causes us to feel dissatisfied with our achievements and ourselves, and to fear failure or criticism. It also leads to procrastination, stress, and burnout. Studies have shown that perfectionism can reduce our happiness by up to 25%. To overcome perfectionism, we can set realistic and flexible goals, celebrate our progress and efforts, or adopt a growth mindset.

Comparison is the habit of measuring ourselves against others in terms of appearance, success, or possessions. Comparison makes us feel envious, inferior, or superior, and erodes our self-confidence and happiness. It also blinds us to our own strengths and uniqueness. Studies have shown that comparison can lower our happiness by up to 20%. To avoid comparison, we can focus on our own values and aspirations, appreciate what we have, or practice gratitude and kindness.

Self-criticism is the habit of judging ourselves harshly or negatively. Self-criticism damages our self-esteem and happiness, and triggers feelings of shame and guilt. It also inhibits our learning
and growth, and increases our risk of depression and anxiety. Studies have shown that self-criticism can decrease our happiness by up to 15%. To replace self-criticism with self-compassion, we can use the strategies mentioned above, or practice positive self-talk.

In conclusion, happiness is not a destination, but a journey. By adopting the habits of happy people, and avoiding the habits of unhappy people, we can increase our happiness levels and enjoy our lives more fully.

Happiness is not a fixed state that we either have or don't have. It is a skill that we can learn and practice, just like any other skill. In this text, we will explore how to apply the science of happiness to our daily lives, and how to make happiness a habit.

The science of happiness is based on the idea that happiness is influenced by both our genes and our environment. Our genes set a range for our potential happiness, but our environment can help us move up or down within that range. This means that we have some control over our happiness, and we can increase it by changing our habits.

One way to change our habits is to create a happiness plan. A happiness plan is a set of activities that we commit to do regularly, that are proven to boost our happiness. These activities can vary depending on our personality, preferences, and goals, but some common examples are:

- **Expressing gratitude:** Gratitude is the feeling of appreciation for what we have and what others do for us. It helps us focus on the positive aspects of our lives, and strengthens our relationships. We can express gratitude by writing a thank-you note, keeping a gratitude journal, or saying thank you more often.

- **Practicing kindness:** Kindness is the act of doing something good for someone else, without expecting anything in return. It makes us feel good about ourselves, and increases our sense of connection and belonging. We can practice kindness by volunteering, donating, complimenting, or helping someone in need.

30

- **Savoring:** Savoring is the act of paying attention to and enjoying the present moment. It helps us appreciate the beauty and joy of life, and reduces stress and anxiety. We can savor by slowing down, using our senses, sharing with others, or reminiscing about positive memories.

- **Meditating:** Meditation is the practice of focusing our attention on a single object, such as our breath, a word, or a sound. It helps us calm our mind, regulate our emotions, and increase our awareness and compassion. We can meditate by following a guided audio, sitting quietly, or walking mindfully.

- **Exercising:** Exercise is the activity of moving our body in a way that improves our physical health and fitness. It also boosts our mood, energy, and self-esteem. We can exercise by doing any physical activity that we enjoy, such as walking, running, dancing, or playing sports.

To create a happiness plan, we need to choose one or more activities that suit our personality, preferences, and goals. We also need to decide how often and when we will do them, and how we will track our progress and evaluate our results. For example, we can use a calendar, a journal, or an app to record when we do the activities, how we feel before and after them, and what challenges or benefits we encounter.

By creating and following a happiness plan, we can make happiness a habit. We can train our brain to look for the positive, rather than the negative aspects of life. We can also increase our resilience and coping skills when we face difficulties or setbacks. We can become happier by changing our habits.

31

# CHAPTER 8: The Practices of Happy People

What do happy people do differently from others? How do they cultivate positive emotions and well-being in their daily lives? In this chapter, we will explore some of the practices that happy people use to enhance their happiness and cope with challenges. These practices are not just random behaviors, but intentional actions that are based on scientific evidence and personal experience. Some of these practices are:

- **Gratitude:** Gratitude is the appreciation of what is valuable and meaningful in one's life. It is a way of recognizing and savoring the good things that happen, as well as expressing thanks to others who have contributed to one's happiness. Gratitude can increase positive emotions, reduce negative emotions, strengthen relationships, and improve physical and mental health. Some ways to practice gratitude are: keeping a gratitude journal, writing thank-you notes, saying grace before meals, or expressing gratitude to someone verbally or nonverbally.

- **Mindfulness:** Mindfulness is the awareness of one's present moment experience, without judgment or distraction. It is a way of paying attention to what is happening in one's body, mind, and environment, with curiosity and openness. Mindfulness can enhance happiness by reducing stress, anxiety, and depression, improving attention and memory, fostering self-compassion and empathy, and increasing happiness and satisfaction. Some ways to practice mindfulness are: meditating, breathing exercises, yoga, or mindful eating.

32

- **Optimism:** Optimism is the expectation that good things will happen in the future, and that one has the ability to influence positive outcomes. It is a way of interpreting events in a favorable way, focusing on the bright side, and seeing challenges as opportunities for growth and learning. Optimism can boost happiness by increasing motivation, resilience, and self-esteem, reducing negative emotions and pessimism, and promoting physical and mental health. Some ways to practice optimism are: setting realistic and attainable goals, visualizing success, reframing negative thoughts, or using affirmations.

- **Kindness:** Kindness is the act of doing something good for someone else, without expecting anything in return. It is a way of showing compassion, generosity, and care for others, as well as oneself. Kindness can enhance happiness by creating positive emotions, such as joy, love, and gratitude, strengthening social bonds and trust, improving self-worth and confidence, and reducing stress and hostility. Some ways to practice kindness are: volunteering, donating, helping a stranger, complimenting someone, or smiling.

- **Flow:** Flow is the state of being fully immersed and engaged in an activity that is challenging but enjoyable. It is a way of finding meaning and fulfillment in one's work or hobbies, by using one's skills and strengths to overcome obstacles and achieve goals. Flow can increase happiness by providing a sense of mastery, autonomy, and purpose, enhancing creativity and productivity, reducing boredom and anxiety, and improving performance and satisfaction. Some ways to experience flow are: choosing activities that match one's interests and abilities, setting clear and immediate feedback, eliminating distractions, or focusing on the process rather than the outcome.

These are just some examples of the practices that happy people use to cultivate positive emotions and well-being. Of course, there are many other practices that can also contribute to happiness, such as humor, forgiveness, exercise, music, or spirituality. The key is to find the practices that suit one's personality, preferences, and circumstances, and to make them a regular part of one's life. By doing so, one can not only increase one's happiness level but also maintain it over time.

# CHAPTER 9: The Skills of Happy People

What are the skills that happy people have in common? How can we learn and improve these skills to enhance our own happiness? In this chapter, we will explore some of the key skills that research has identified as essential for happiness, such as gratitude, optimism, resilience, mindfulness, compassion, and self-regulation. We will also discuss how to practice these skills in our daily lives and overcome the obstacles that may prevent us from developing them.

Gratitude is the skill of appreciating what we have and expressing our thanks to others. Gratitude helps us to focus on the positive aspects of our lives and to recognize the sources of our happiness. Gratitude also strengthens our relationships, as it makes us more generous, kind, and supportive. To cultivate gratitude, we can keep a gratitude journal, write thank-you notes, share our gratitude with others, and practice gratitude meditation.

Optimism is the skill of expecting positive outcomes and having a hopeful attitude. Optimism helps us to cope with challenges, to see opportunities in difficulties, and to pursue our goals with confidence. Optimism also boosts our health, as it reduces stress, enhances immunity, and promotes longevity. To cultivate optimism, we can reframe negative thoughts, visualize positive scenarios, set realistic and achievable goals, and celebrate our successes.

Resilience is the skill of bouncing back from adversity and overcoming obstacles. Resilience helps us to adapt to changing circumstances, to learn from failures, and to grow from hardships. Resilience also fosters our well-being, as it increases our self-esteem, self-efficacy, and satisfaction. To cultivate resilience, we can embrace challenges, seek support, practice self-compassion, and find meaning in difficulties.

34

Mindfulness is the skill of paying attention to the present moment with curiosity and openness. Mindfulness helps us to savor the joys of life, to reduce distractions, and to regulate our emotions. Mindfulness also enhances our mental health, as it lowers anxiety, depression, and rumination. To cultivate mindfulness, we can practice meditation, yoga, breathing exercises, or any activity that requires focused attention.

Compassion is the skill of feeling for others and acting to alleviate their suffering. Compassion helps us to connect with others, to empathize with their feelings, and to contribute to their well-being. Compassion also benefits ourselves, as it activates the reward centers in our brain, reduces inflammation in our body, and increases happiness hormones in our blood. To cultivate compassion, we can practice loving-kindness meditation, perform acts of kindness, volunteer for a cause, or join a compassion training program.

Self-regulation is the skill of managing our thoughts, emotions, and behaviors in accordance with our values and goals. Self-regulation helps us to align our actions with our intentions, to resist temptations, and to persist in the face of difficulties. Self-regulation also improves our performance, as it enhances our focus, motivation, and productivity. To cultivate self-regulation, we can set SMART goals (specific, measurable, attainable, relevant, and time-bound), monitor our progress, use feedback loops (plan-do-check-act), reward ourselves for achievements, and use if-then plans (if situation X occurs, then I will do Y).

These are some of the skills that happy people have mastered or are working on improving. Of course, there are many other skills that can contribute to happiness, such as creativity, curiosity, humor, and wisdom. The important thing is to find out what works for you and to practice it regularly.

As Aristotle said, "We are what we repeatedly do. Excellence, then, is not an act, but a habit."

# CHAPTER 10: The Strategies of Happy People

What are the strategies that happy people use to maintain and enhance their happiness? In this chapter, we will explore some of the most effective and evidence-based strategies that have been identified by happiness science. These strategies are not one-size-fits-all solutions, but rather tools that can be adapted and applied to different situations and contexts. Some of these strategies may seem obvious or intuitive, while others may require more effort or practice. However, they all share a common goal: to help us cultivate positive emotions and well-being in our lives.

The first strategy is to set and pursue meaningful goals. Goals are the targets or outcomes that we want to achieve in various domains of our lives, such as work, education, health, relationships, hobbies, etc. Goals can provide us with a sense of direction, purpose, challenge, and achievement. They can also motivate us to learn new skills, overcome obstacles, and grow as individuals. However, not all goals are equally beneficial for our happiness. Happiness science suggests that the best goals are those that are:

- **Self-concordant:** They reflect our true interests, values, and passions, rather than external pressures or expectations.
- **Specific:** They have clear and measurable criteria for success, rather than vague or abstract standards.
- **Challenging:** They stretch our abilities and require some effort, but not beyond our capabilities or resources.
- **Flexible:** They can be adjusted or revised according to changing circumstances or feedback.

36

- **Balanced:** They cover different areas of our lives and do not compromise our other needs or values.

By setting and pursuing self-concordant, specific, challenging, flexible, and balanced goals, we can increase our chances of achieving them and experiencing positive emotions along the way. We can also enhance our self-efficacy, self-esteem, and self-worth, which are important components of happiness.

The second strategy is to practice gratitude. Gratitude is the feeling of appreciation or thankfulness for the benefits or blessings that we receive from others or from life in general. Gratitude can help us recognize and savor the positive aspects of our lives, rather than taking them for granted or focusing on the negative ones. Gratitude can also strengthen our social bonds, by expressing our appreciation to those who support us or contribute to our well-being. Gratitude can also foster a sense of abundance, by acknowledging that we have enough or more than enough of what we need or want.

Happiness science suggests that gratitude can be cultivated through various practices, such as:

- **Keeping a gratitude journal:** Writing down three to five things that we are grateful for each day or week.
- **Writing a gratitude letter:** Writing a letter to someone who has made a positive difference in our lives, expressing our gratitude and appreciation for their actions or qualities.
- **Saying thank you:** Verbally expressing our gratitude to others for their kindness or generosity, either in person or through phone calls, messages, emails, etc.
- **Counting blessings:** Mentally listing the things that we are grateful for in a given situation or context.
- **Savoring:** Paying attention to and enjoying the positive experiences or sensations that we encounter in our daily lives.

By practicing gratitude regularly, we can increase our positive emotions and well-being, as well as reduce our negative emotions and stress. We can also enhance our optimism, satisfaction, and happiness with life.

The third strategy is to cultivate optimism. Optimism is the tendency to expect positive outcomes or to view the future with hope and confidence. Optimism can help us cope with challenges and difficulties, by focusing on the opportunities or solutions rather than the problems or threats. Optimism can also motivate us to take action and pursue our goals, by believing in our abilities and chances of success. Optimism can also foster a sense of resilience, by learning from failures or setbacks rather than giving up or blaming ourselves.

Happiness science suggests that optimism can be cultivated through various practices, such as:

- **Reframing**: Changing the way we interpret or evaluate a situation or event from a negative to a positive perspective.
- **Best possible self**: Imagining ourselves in the future having achieved our goals and living our ideal life.
- **Positive affirmations**: Repeating positive statements or phrases that reflect our strengths, values, or aspirations.
- **Hopeful thinking**: Generating multiple pathways or plans to achieve our goals and anticipating potential obstacles or difficulties.
- **Self-compassion**: Treating ourselves with kindness and understanding when we face challenges or make mistakes.

One of the benefits of cultivating optimism regularly is that it can improve your physical and mental health. Optimism is a positive attitude that expects good things to happen in the future and sees challenges as opportunities to learn. According to research, optimists are more likely to maintain better physical health than pessimists, as they have lower stress levels, stronger immune systems, and lower risk of chronic diseases. Optimists are also less prone to anxiety and depression, as they cope better with adversity and have more confidence in their abilities. Optimism can also enhance your cognitive functions and memory, as it makes you more attentive to positive information and more likely to recall pleasant experiences. By cultivating optimism regularly, you can also increase your level of physical activity, as you will be more motivated to explore the world and take care of yourself. Optimism can also boost your achievement and persistence, as you will set higher goals, work harder, and overcome obstacles more easily. Optimism can also improve your relationships, as you will be more supportive, cooperative, and compassionate with others. Cultivating optimism regularly can have many benefits for your well-being and happiness.

# CHAPTER 11: The Challenges of Happiness

Happiness is not a constant state of bliss that can be achieved once and for all. Happiness is a dynamic and complex phenomenon that requires constant effort, adaptation, and resilience. Happiness is also not a guarantee that everything will go smoothly in life. Happiness is often challenged by various factors, such as stress, adversity, loss, conflict, uncertainty, and change. In this chapter, we will explore some of the common challenges that people face in their pursuit of happiness, and how they can cope with them effectively.

One of the major challenges of happiness is stress. Stress is a natural and inevitable response to the demands and pressures of life. Stress can have positive effects, such as motivating us to perform better, enhancing our learning and memory, and strengthening our immune system. However, when stress is excessive, chronic, or unmanageable, it can have negative effects on our physical and mental health, such as causing fatigue, insomnia, headaches, anxiety, depression, and cardiovascular diseases. Stress can also interfere with our happiness by reducing our positive emotions, impairing our cognitive abilities, weakening our social relationships, and lowering our self-esteem.

How can we deal with stress in a healthy way? One of the most effective ways is to practice relaxation techniques, such as deep breathing, progressive muscle relaxation, meditation, yoga, tai chi, or biofeedback. Relaxation techniques can help us calm our nervous system, lower our blood pressure and heart rate, reduce our muscle tension and pain, and enhance our mood and well-being. Another way to cope with stress is to adopt a positive mindset, such as optimism, gratitude, humor, or acceptance. A positive mindset can help us see the bright side of situations, appreciate what we have, laugh at ourselves and our problems, or accept what we

39

cannot change. A third way to manage stress is to seek social support from our family, friends, colleagues, or professionals. Social support can provide us with emotional comfort,
practical assistance, informational guidance, or feedback. Social support can also buffer us from the negative effects of stress by increasing our sense of belonging, trust, and self-worth.

To illustrate these ways of coping with stress more concretely, let us consider some examples from real life. One example is the story of Viktor Frankl, a psychiatrist who survived the Nazi concentration camps during World War II. Frankl used relaxation techniques to cope with the physical hardships and torture he endured in the camps. He also adopted a positive mindset by finding meaning in his suffering and envisioning his future goals. He also sought social support from his fellow prisoners and helped them cope as well. Frankl's experience shows that even in the most extreme situations of stress and adversity, we can still find ways to preserve our happiness and dignity.

Another example is the story of Malala Yousafzai, a Pakistani activist who was shot by the Taliban for advocating for girls' education. Malala used relaxation techniques to recover from her injuries and trauma. She also adopted a positive mindset by forgiving her attackers and continuing her mission. She also sought social support from her family, friends, and the international community who supported her cause. Malala's experience shows that even in the face of violence and oppression, we can still find ways to pursue our happiness and values.

A third example is the story of J.K. Rowling, a British author who wrote the Harry Potter series. Rowling used relaxation techniques to cope with the stress of being a single mother living in poverty. She also adopted a positive mindset by using her imagination and creativity to write her stories. She also sought social support from her daughter, her agent, and her readers who loved her books. Rowling's experience shows that even in the midst of hardship and uncertainty, we can still find ways to express our happiness and talents.

Another challenge of happiness is adversity. Adversity is any situation or event that causes stress, hardship, or suffering. It can be personal, such as illness, loss, or trauma, or external, such as war, poverty, or discrimination. Adversity can affect our happiness in different ways, depending on how we cope with it. Some people may become depressed, anxious, or hopeless when faced with adversity, while others may find meaning, resilience, or growth.

The way we respond to adversity is influenced by many factors, such as our personality, beliefs, values, goals, social support, and coping skills. Some of these factors are innate, while others can be learned or developed. For example, some people may have a positive outlook on life that helps them see the silver lining in every situation, while others may learn to practice gratitude, optimism, or mindfulness to enhance their well-being. Similarly, some people may have a strong sense of purpose that motivates them to overcome challenges, while others may seek help from friends, family, or professionals to cope with their difficulties.

Adversity can also be a source of happiness if we use it as an opportunity to grow and improve ourselves. Research has shown that some people experience post-traumatic growth after going through traumatic events. This means that they report positive changes in their self-perception, relationships, spirituality, or life priorities as a result of their adversity. They may also develop new skills, strengths, or perspectives that help them cope better with future challenges. Post-traumatic growth does not mean that people are happy about their trauma or that they forget their pain. Rather, it means that they find a way to transform their suffering into something meaningful and valuable.

Therefore, adversity is not necessarily an obstacle to happiness, but rather a challenge that can be overcome with the right mindset and resources. By facing our adversity with courage, compassion, and creativity, we can not only survive but also thrive and flourish.

# CHAPTER 12: The Paradoxes of Happiness

Happiness is a complex and elusive phenomenon that has fascinated philosophers, scientists, and ordinary people for centuries. But as much as we may strive to understand and achieve happiness, there are some paradoxes that seem to challenge our efforts and expectations. In this chapter, we will explore some of these paradoxes and how they can help us to deepen our appreciation and awareness of happiness.

One paradox of happiness is that it is not always correlated with objective indicators of well-being, such as income, health, or education. Some people may be very happy despite having low levels of these factors, while others may be unhappy despite having high levels of them. This suggests that happiness is not a fixed state that depends on external circumstances, but rather a dynamic and subjective experience that depends on internal factors, such as values, beliefs, goals, and attitudes.

Another paradox of happiness is that it is not always the result of positive events or outcomes, but sometimes the cause of them. For example, some studies have shown that happy people are more likely to be successful in various domains of life, such as work, relationships, or health. This implies that happiness is not only a consequence of success, but also a catalyst for it. Happiness may enhance our motivation, creativity, productivity, resilience, and social skills, which in turn may lead to more positive outcomes.

A third paradox of happiness is that it is not always increased by getting what we want, but sometimes by wanting what we have. This means that happiness is not only determined by the gap between our desires and our reality, but also by the way we perceive and appreciate our reality. Happiness may be enhanced by cultivating

42

gratitude, satisfaction, and contentment with what we already have, rather than constantly pursuing more or better things.

A fourth paradox of happiness is that it is not always diminished by negative events or emotions, but sometimes by positive ones. This implies that happiness is not only threatened by the presence of pain, sadness, or fear, but also by the absence of meaning, purpose, or growth. Happiness may be enriched by embracing the full spectrum of human emotions and experiences, both pleasant and unpleasant, as opportunities for learning and transformation.

A fifth paradox of happiness is that it is not always shared by similar people or cultures, but sometimes by different ones. This indicates that happiness is not only influenced by the commonalities among human beings, such as universal needs or values, but also by the diversity among them, such as individual preferences or cultural norms. Happiness may be fostered by respecting and celebrating the uniqueness and variety of human expressions and perspectives on happiness.

These paradoxes of happiness are not contradictions or obstacles to happiness, but rather invitations to explore and expand our understanding and practice of happiness. They remind us that happiness is not a simple or static phenomenon, but a complex and dynamic one. They challenge us to question our assumptions and expectations about happiness, and to discover new ways of experiencing and expressing it.

# CHAPTER 13: The Myths of Happiness

Happiness is a complex and multifaceted phenomenon that has been studied by scientists from various disciplines. However, despite the advances in happiness research, there are still many misconceptions and myths about happiness that persist in the popular culture and media. In this chapter, we will examine some of the most common myths of happiness and explain why they are not supported by scientific evidence. We will also discuss how these myths can interfere with our happiness and well-being, and how we can overcome them by adopting a more realistic and evidence-based perspective on happiness.

**Myth 1: Happiness is a destination**
One of the most prevalent myths of happiness is that happiness is a destination that we can reach once we achieve certain goals, such as getting a promotion, finding a partner, buying a house, or having children. This myth implies that happiness is something that we can pursue and attain, and that it depends on external circumstances and achievements. However, this myth is contradicted by the findings of happiness research, which show that happiness is not a static state, but a dynamic process that involves constant fluctuations and adaptations. Happiness is not something that we can chase and capture, but something that we can cultivate and experience in the present moment.

Moreover, this myth ignores the fact that happiness is influenced by many factors beyond our control, such as our genes, personality, temperament, and life events. Happiness is also subject to hedonic adaptation, which means that we tend to get used to the positive changes in our lives and return to our baseline level of happiness over time. Therefore, achieving our goals may not bring us lasting happiness, but only temporary satisfaction. In fact, some studies have found that pursuing extrinsic goals, such as money, fame, or status, can actually reduce our happiness and well-

44

being, because they can distract us from more meaningful and fulfilling activities, such as developing our skills, expressing our creativity, or connecting with others.

The alternative to this myth is to view happiness as a journey, rather than a destination. Happiness is not something that we can find at the end of the road, but something that we can enjoy along the way. Happiness is not dependent on what we have or what we do, but on how we perceive and appreciate what we have and what we do. Happiness is not a fixed outcome, but a flexible attitude that allows us to cope with challenges and embrace opportunities. Happiness is not a matter of chance, but a matter of choice.

### Myth 2: Happiness is the same for everyone

Another common myth of happiness is that happiness is the same for everyone, and that there is a universal formula or recipe for happiness that applies to all people. This myth assumes that happiness is a one-size-fits-all concept that can be measured and compared across individuals and cultures. However, this myth overlooks the fact that happiness is a subjective and personal experience that varies depending on our preferences, values, beliefs, expectations, and goals. Happiness is not a single dimension, but a multidimensional construct that encompasses different aspects of our lives, such as our emotions, thoughts, behaviors, relationships, health, work, leisure, spirituality, and so on.

Furthermore, this myth disregards the fact that happiness is influenced by our cultural background and context, which shape our definitions and expressions of happiness. Happiness is not a universal phenomenon, but a relative and contextual one. Different cultures may have different conceptions and indicators of happiness, such as harmony, balance, contentment, joyfulness or peace. Different cultures may also have different norms and practices for pursuing and displaying happiness, such as individualism or collectivism, optimism or realism,
extraversion or introversion, and so on.

The alternative to this myth is to recognize that happiness is a diverse and individualized experience that reflects our unique personality, values, and circumstances. Happiness is not something that we can copy or imitate from others, but something that we can discover and create for ourselves. Happiness is not something that we can quantify or rank, but something that we can qualify and appreciate. Happiness is not a standard or norm, but an expression of our authenticity and diversity.

### Myth 3: Happiness depends on external factors.

45

Some people believe that happiness is determined by factors outside their control, such as luck, genes, or fate. While these factors may influence happiness to some extent, they are not the main determinants. Happiness depends largely on how we interpret and respond to our experiences, and how we cultivate positive emotions and relationships. Happiness is not something that happens to us, but something that we make happen.

**Myth 4: Happiness is the absence of negative emotions.**
Some people think that happiness means feeling good all the time, and avoiding any negative emotions such as sadness, anger, or fear. However, research shows that happiness is not the absence of negative emotions, but the presence of positive emotions. Negative emotions are natural and inevitable parts of life, and they can serve important functions such as signaling a problem, motivating a change, or enhancing empathy. Happiness is not about denying or suppressing negative emotions, but about embracing and learning from them.

These myths of happiness can interfere with our happiness and well-being by creating unrealistic expectations, limiting our choices, or preventing us from appreciating what we have. We can overcome these myths by adopting a more realistic and evidence-based perspective on happiness, which recognizes that happiness is a complex and multifaceted construct that requires ongoing effort and attention.

# CHAPTER 14: The Measurement of Happiness

How do we know if we are happy? How can we measure something as subjective and complex as happiness? These are some of the questions that happiness researchers have to face when they try to study and quantify happiness. In this chapter, we will explore the different methods and tools that scientists use to measure happiness, as well as the advantages and limitations of each approach.

One of the most common and simple ways to measure happiness is to ask people directly how happy they are. This is called self-report, and it involves using surveys, questionnaires, interviews, or diaries to collect data from individuals about their subjective well-being. Subjective well-being is a term that encompasses how people evaluate their own lives in terms of satisfaction, positive emotions, and negative emotions. Some of the most widely used self-report measures of subjective well-being are:

- The Satisfaction with Life Scale (SWLS), which asks people to rate their agreement with five statements about their overall satisfaction with life, such as "In most ways my life is close to my ideal".

- The Positive and Negative Affect Schedule (PANAS), which asks people to indicate how often they have experienced 20 different emotions (10 positive and 10 negative) in a given time period, such as "interested", "irritable", or "proud".

- The Subjective Happiness Scale (SHS), which asks people to rate their agreement with four statements about their general happiness, such as "I consider myself a happy person".

47

- The Day Reconstruction Method (DRM), which asks people to reconstruct their previous day by dividing it into episodes and reporting how they spent their time, who they were with, and how they felt during each episode.

Self-report measures have the advantage of being easy to administer, inexpensive, and flexible. They also capture the personal and subjective nature of happiness, which may not be accessible by other methods. However, self-report measures also have some drawbacks, such as:

- They rely on people's memory and honesty, which may be biased or inaccurate.
- They may be influenced by social desirability, mood, or context effects, which may affect how people respond to the questions.
- They may not capture the full complexity and diversity of happiness, which may involve more than just satisfaction and emotions.
- They may not be comparable across different cultures, languages, or groups of people, who may have different definitions and expressions of happiness.

Another way to measure happiness is to observe people's behavior and physiology. This is called objective measurement, and it involves using sensors, devices, or experiments to collect data from individuals about their biological or psychological indicators of happiness. Some of the most commonly used objective measures of happiness are:

- Facial expressions, which are the movements of the muscles in the face that reflect different emotions. Researchers can use software or trained coders to analyze facial expressions from photos or videos and infer the emotional state of the person.

- Voice analysis, which is the examination of the acoustic features of the voice that convey different emotions. Researchers can use software or trained coders to analyze voice recordings and infer the emotional state of the person.

- Brain activity, which is the electrical or metabolic activity of the brain that corresponds to different mental processes. Researchers can use techniques such as electroencephalography (EEG) or functional magnetic resonance imaging (fMRI) to measure brain activity from electrodes or scanners and infer the cognitive or affective state of the person.

48

- Heart rate variability (HRV), which is the variation in the time interval between heartbeats that reflects the balance between the sympathetic and parasympathetic nervous systems. Researchers can use devices such as chest straps or wristbands to measure HRV from heart signals and infer the stress or relaxation level of the person.

Objective measures have the advantage of being more reliable, valid, and precise than self-report measures. They also capture the biological and psychological aspects of happiness, which may not be fully reported by individuals. However, objective measures also have some limitations, such as:

- They are more invasive, expensive, and complex than self-report measures. They may require specialized equipment, training, or consent from participants.
- They may not reflect the subjective experience of happiness, which may not be fully captured by behavior or physiology.
- They may be influenced by confounding factors, such as noise, temperature, or medication, which may affect the behavior or physiology of participants.
- They may not be generalizable across different situations, tasks, or stimuli, which may elicit different responses from participants.

As we can see, there is no single or perfect way to measure happiness. Each method has its strengths and weaknesses, and each one provides a different perspective on happiness. Therefore, researchers often use a combination of methods to obtain a more comprehensive and accurate picture of happiness. By measuring happiness in multiple ways, we can gain a deeper understanding of what makes us happy and how we can enhance our well-being.

# CHAPTER 15: The Science of Happiness

In the previous chapters, we have explored the various aspects of happiness, from its biological, psychological, social, environmental, spiritual, and behavioral dimensions, to its challenges, paradoxes, myths, and measurement. We have also learned about the habits, practices, skills, and strategies that happy people use to cultivate positive emotions and well-being in their lives. But what is the science behind all these findings? How do researchers study happiness and what methods do they use? What are the benefits and limitations of happiness science? And how can we apply the scientific knowledge of happiness to our own lives and to the world around us? These are some of the questions that we will address in this chapter.

The science of happiness is a relatively new and interdisciplinary field that draws from various disciplines such as psychology, neuroscience, sociology, economics, philosophy, and more. It is also known as positive psychology, which is the scientific study of human flourishing and optimal functioning. Positive psychology focuses on the strengths and virtues that enable individuals and communities to thrive, rather than on the problems and disorders that cause suffering. Positive psychology was founded by Martin Seligman in 1998, when he became the president of the American Psychological Association and declared that psychology should not only aim to heal what is wrong with people, but also to enhance what is right with them.

One of the main goals of positive psychology is to identify and measure the factors that contribute to happiness and well-being. To do this, researchers use various methods such as surveys, experiments, interviews, observations, and more. They also use different tools to assess happiness and well-being, such as self-reports, physiological measures, behavioral indicators, and objective indicators. For example, self-reports are subjective evaluations of one's own happiness and well-being, such as life satisfaction, positive affect, meaning in life, etc. Physiological measures are objective indicators of one's bodily state, such as heart rate, blood pressure, cortisol levels, etc. Behavioral indicators are observable actions that reflect one's happiness and well-being, such as smiling, laughing, helping others, etc. Objective indicators are external factors that influence one's happiness and well-being, such as income, education, health, etc.

The science of happiness has many benefits for individuals and society. It can help us understand ourselves better and discover what makes us happy and fulfilled. It can also help us improve our mental and physical health, enhance our relationships, increase our productivity and creativity, and foster our resilience and coping skills. Moreover, it can help us promote positive change in our communities and in the world by applying the principles of happiness science to various domains such as education, health care, business, politics, etc.

The science of happiness is a multidisciplinary field that explores the factors that contribute to human well-being and flourishing. It draws on insights from psychology, neuroscience, sociology, economics, and other domains to understand how people can experience more positive emotions, engagement, meaning, and accomplishment in their lives. However, the science of happiness also has some limitations that we should be aware of. One of them is the challenge of measuring happiness accurately and reliably. Happiness is a complex and subjective phenomenon that can be influenced by many factors, such as culture, personality, expectations, and context. Different measures of happiness, such as self-reports, physiological indicators, cognitive tests, or behavioral observations, may capture different aspects of happiness or be affected by different sources of error or bias. Moreover, happiness measures may not be comparable across individuals or groups, unless they are properly calibrated to account for differences in interpretation, expression, or scaling of happiness ratings. Therefore, researchers and practitioners need to be cautious and critical when using and interpreting happiness measures, and acknowledge the uncertainty and variability that may exist in the data.

# CHAPTER 16: The Application of Happiness Science

In the previous chapters, we have explored the science of happiness from various perspectives, such as biology, psychology, sociology, spirituality, and more. We have learned about the factors that influence our happiness, the habits, practices, skills, and strategies that can enhance our happiness, and the challenges, paradoxes, myths, and measurements of happiness. We have also seen how happiness science is a growing and evolving field that aims to understand and promote human well-being.

But how can we apply the insights and findings of happiness science to our own lives and to the lives of others? How can we use happiness science to improve our personal and professional well-being, as well as the well-being of our families, communities, and societies? How can we translate happiness science into practical and effective interventions that can make a positive difference in the world?

In this chapter, we will address these questions and explore some of the ways that happiness science can be applied in various domains and contexts. We will look at some examples of how happiness science has been used to design and implement programs, policies, and practices that aim to increase happiness and well-being at different levels: individual, interpersonal, organizational, and societal. We will also discuss some of the challenges and limitations of applying happiness science, as well as some of the ethical and moral issues that arise from it. Finally, we will offer some suggestions and recommendations on how to apply happiness science in a responsible and beneficial way.

The main objectives of this chapter are:

- To provide an overview of the application of happiness science in different domains and contexts
- To illustrate some examples of how happiness science has been used to create positive change in the world
- To discuss some of the challenges and limitations of applying happiness science
- To address some of the ethical and moral issues related to applying happiness science
- To offer some suggestions and recommendations on how to apply happiness science effectively and responsibly

**To provide an overview of the application of happiness science in different domains and contexts**

Happiness science is the interdisciplinary study of what makes people and societies flourish and thrive. It draws on insights from psychology, economics, sociology, neuroscience, and other fields to measure and enhance well-being at multiple levels. Happiness science has been applied in various domains and contexts, such as education, health, work, public policy, and international development. Some examples of how happiness science is used in these areas are:

- In education, happiness science can help design curricula and pedagogies that foster not only academic achievement but also social and emotional skills, resilience, creativity, and positive relationships among students and teachers.

- In health, happiness science can inform interventions and policies that promote physical and mental health, prevent and treat diseases, and support people with chronic conditions or disabilities to live fulfilling lives.

- In work, happiness science can help create organizational cultures and practices that enhance employee engagement, productivity, satisfaction, and well-being, as well as reduce stress, burnout, and turnover.

- In public policy, happiness science can provide indicators and tools to measure and improve the quality of life of citizens, such as the Gross National Happiness index or the World Happiness Report. It can also help evaluate the impact of policies on well-being and incorporate well-being as a criterion for decision-making.

53

- In international development, happiness science can help design and implement programs and projects that address the needs and aspirations of people in different contexts and cultures, such as poverty alleviation, human rights, gender equality, environmental sustainability, and peacebuilding.

**To illustrate some examples of how happiness science has been used to create positive change in the world**

Happiness science is the study of what makes people happy and how to enhance well-being. It is based on the idea that happiness is not just a fleeting emotion, but a skill that can be cultivated and practiced. Happiness science has been used to create positive change in the world in various ways, such as:

- **Improving mental health and resilience.** Happiness science has shown that gratitude, optimism, mindfulness, and self-compassion are some of the factors that can boost happiness and protect against stress, depression, and anxiety. These practices can also help people cope with adversity, trauma, and loss. For example, a study by Seligman et al. (2005) found that teaching positive psychology interventions to soldiers before deployment reduced their risk of developing post-traumatic stress disorder.

- **Enhancing social relationships and community.** Happiness science has shown that happiness is contagious and that social connections are vital for well-being. People who are happy tend to spread their positive emotions to others, creating a virtuous cycle of happiness. People who have strong social ties also tend to be happier, healthier, and more satisfied with their lives. For example, a study by Fowler and Christakis (2008) found that having a happy friend increased one's own happiness by 15%, while having a happy neighbor increased it by 34%.

- **Promoting prosocial behavior and altruism.** Happiness science has shown that happiness is not only good for oneself, but also for others. People who are happy tend to be more generous, cooperative, helpful, and compassionate. They also tend to care more about social justice, human rights, and environmental issues. For example, a study by Aknin et al. (2013) found that spending money on others increased happiness more than spending money on oneself, across 136 countries.

- **Fostering creativity and innovation.** Happiness science has shown that happiness can enhance cognitive abilities, such as memory, attention, learning, and problem-solving. People who are happy tend to be more curious, open-minded, flexible, and original. They also tend to perform better at work, school, and other domains. For example, a study by Amabile et al. (2005) found that positive emotions increased creativity among professionals in various fields.

These are just some of the examples of how happiness science has been used to create positive change in the world. Happiness science is not only a fascinating field of research, but also a powerful tool for improving individual and collective well-being.

**To discuss some of the challenges and limitations of applying happiness science**

Happiness science is the interdisciplinary study of what makes people happy and how to promote well-being in individuals and societies. However, applying happiness science to real-world problems is not without challenges and limitations. Some of these are:

- Happiness is a subjective and multidimensional concept that is difficult to measure and compare across different contexts and cultures. Different people may have different definitions, expectations, and preferences for happiness, which may not be captured by standardized scales or indicators.

- Happiness science is often based on self-reported data, which may be influenced by various biases, such as social desirability, memory, mood, or framing effects. Self-reported data may also not reflect actual behavior or outcomes, such as health, productivity, or social relationships.

- Happiness science may not account for the trade-offs, costs, and unintended consequences of pursuing or promoting happiness. For example, some interventions or policies that aim to increase happiness may have negative effects on other aspects of well-being, such as autonomy, justice, or diversity. Alternatively, some sources of happiness may be unsustainable or harmful in the long term, such as consumerism, hedonism, or addiction.

- Happiness science may not be able to address the structural and systemic factors that affect happiness, such as poverty, inequality, oppression, or

55

    violence. These factors may limit the opportunities and choices of individuals and groups to pursue happiness, and may require more radical and collective solutions than individual or psychological ones.

- Happiness science may face ethical and moral dilemmas when applying its findings and recommendations to different contexts and populations. For example, some interventions or policies that aim to increase happiness may be paternalistic, coercive, or manipulative, violating the autonomy and dignity of the people involved. Alternatively, some interventions or policies that aim to increase happiness may be unfair, unjust, or discriminatory, favoring some groups over others.

These are some of the challenges and limitations of applying happiness science that need to be acknowledged and addressed by researchers, practitioners, and policymakers who are interested in this field.

**To address some of the ethical and moral issues related to applying happiness science**

One of the challenges of applying happiness science is to address some of the ethical and moral issues that may arise from its use. Happiness science is the interdisciplinary study of what makes humans and other animals happy, and how to promote well-being for individuals and societies. It draws on insights from psychology, neuroscience, economics, philosophy, and other fields. However, happiness science is not value-neutral, and it may have implications for how we treat ourselves, others, and the environment.

Some of the ethical and moral issues related to applying happiness science are:

- **How do we define and measure happiness?** Happiness is a subjective experience that may vary across cultures, contexts, and individuals. There is no single or objective way to quantify happiness, and different methods may yield different results. For example, some people may report high levels of life satisfaction, but low levels of positive emotions, or vice versa. Some people may value happiness more than others, or have different preferences for how to achieve it. How do we account for these differences and complexities when we apply happiness science?

- **How do we balance individual and collective happiness?** Happiness science may suggest ways to enhance individual well-being, such as pursuing meaningful goals, cultivating positive relationships, or practicing gratitude. However, these strategies may not always align with the interests or values of other people or groups. For example, some people may pursue happiness at the expense of others, or some groups may impose their views of happiness on others. How do we ensure that applying happiness science does not harm or oppress anyone, and that it respects diversity and autonomy?

- **How do we weigh happiness against other moral values?** Happiness is not the only thing that matters ethically. There may be situations where maximizing happiness conflicts with other moral principles, such as justice, fairness, rights, or duties. For example, some forms of animal testing may increase human happiness by advancing medical research, but they may also cause animal suffering. Some forms of genetic engineering may enhance human happiness by eliminating diseases or disabilities, but they may also raise concerns about human dignity or equality. How do we decide which values take priority when we apply happiness science?

- **How do we ensure the responsible use of happiness science?** Happiness science may offer powerful tools to influence human behavior and well-being, such as neurostimulation, psychopharmacology, or nudging. However, these tools may also pose risks of misuse or abuse by individuals, organizations, or governments. For example, some people may become addicted to artificial sources of happiness, or lose their authenticity or autonomy. Some organizations or governments may manipulate people's emotions or preferences for their own benefit. How do we regulate and monitor the use of happiness science to prevent harm or coercion?

These are some of the ethical and moral issues related to applying happiness science that require careful consideration and deliberation. Applying happiness science is not just a matter of finding out what works, but also of asking why it works, for whom it works, and at what cost it works. Happiness science should not be seen as a panacea or a prescription, but as a source of information and inspiration that can help us make better decisions for ourselves and others.

**To offer some suggestions and recommendations on how to apply happiness science effectively and responsibly**

Happiness science is the study of what makes people happy and how to improve well-being. It is a multidisciplinary field that draws on psychology, economics, sociology, neuroscience, and other disciplines. Happiness science can offer valuable insights and tools for individuals, organizations, and policymakers who want to enhance happiness and quality of life. However, happiness science also comes with some challenges and limitations that need to be considered and addressed. Here are some suggestions and recommendations on how to apply happiness science effectively and responsibly:

- **Be aware of the complexity and diversity of happiness.** Happiness is not a simple or universal concept. It can be defined and measured in different ways, such as life satisfaction, positive emotions, meaning, or flourishing. Moreover, happiness can vary across cultures, contexts, and individuals. What makes one person happy may not make another person happy. Therefore, when applying happiness science, it is important to be respectful and sensitive to the different perspectives and preferences of people and groups.

- **Be critical and cautious of the evidence and claims.** Happiness science is a relatively new and evolving field that relies on various methods and sources of data. Some of the findings and recommendations may not be conclusive, reliable, or generalizable. For example, some studies may use self-reported measures of happiness that are prone to biases and errors. Some interventions may work well in controlled settings but not in real-world situations. Some effects may be short-lived or moderated by other factors. Therefore, when applying happiness science, it is important to evaluate the quality and validity of the evidence and claims, and to avoid overconfidence and oversimplification.

- **Be ethical and respectful of the autonomy and dignity of people.** Happiness science can have positive impacts on people's well-being, but it can also have negative or unintended consequences if used inappropriately or coercively. For example, some interventions may infringe on people's privacy, freedom, or diversity. Some policies may impose happiness as a norm or a duty that neglects or oppresses other values or goals. Some practices may manipulate or exploit people's emotions or behaviors for ulterior motives. Therefore, when applying happiness science, it is important to adhere to ethical principles and respect the autonomy and dignity of people.

58

# CHAPTER 17: The Promotion of Happiness Science

Happiness is not only a personal goal, but also a social good. The science of happiness has shown that happy people are more productive, creative, healthy, resilient, altruistic, and cooperative. They also contribute to the well-being of their families, communities, and societies. Therefore, promoting happiness science is not only beneficial for individuals, but also for the collective welfare of humanity.

But how can we promote happiness science? How can we spread the knowledge and practice of happiness to more people and places? How can we make happiness science accessible, relevant, and engaging for diverse audiences and contexts? How can we overcome the barriers and challenges that prevent people from learning and applying happiness science? How can we evaluate the impact and effectiveness of happiness science promotion?

In this chapter, we will explore these questions and offer some suggestions and examples of how to promote happiness science in various domains and settings. We will discuss how to promote happiness science in education, health care, work, media, policy, and culture. We will also highlight some of the best practices and principles of happiness science promotion, such as using evidence-based methods, tailoring to the needs and preferences of the target audience, involving multiple stakeholders, fostering collaboration and community, and ensuring sustainability and scalability.

## How can we promote happiness science?

Happiness is a universal human desire, but how can we achieve it? Is there a science behind happiness that can help us understand and improve our well-being? In this text, we will explore some of the main findings and applications of the science of happiness, also known as positive psychology.

The science of happiness is a relatively new field of research that examines the factors and practices that contribute to a happy and meaningful life. It draws from various disciplines, such as psychology, neuroscience, evolutionary biology, and sociology, to investigate how people can flourish and thrive in different contexts.

One of the key insights from the science of happiness is that happiness is not just a result of external circumstances, but also a product of our internal choices and actions. Happiness is not something that happens to us, but something that we can cultivate and enhance through our habits, mindsets, and behaviors.

Some of the evidence-based strategies that the science of happiness suggests are:

- **Practicing gratitude**: Gratitude is the appreciation of what is valuable and meaningful in our lives. It helps us savor the positive aspects of our experiences, cope with stress, and strengthen our relationships. Research shows that expressing gratitude regularly can boost our happiness, health, and resilience.

- **Cultivating optimism**: Optimism is the tendency to expect positive outcomes and view challenges as opportunities for growth. It helps us cope with adversity, pursue our goals, and maintain a positive outlook on life. Research shows that optimism can enhance our happiness, well-being, and performance.

- **Fostering social connections**: Social connections are the relationships we have with others, such as family, friends, colleagues, and community members. They provide us with support, belonging, and meaning. Research shows that social connections are one of the strongest predictors of happiness and well-being.

- **Engaging in flow activities**: Flow is the state of being fully immersed and absorbed in an activity that challenges our skills and matches our interests. It helps us enjoy the process of doing something, rather than focusing on the outcome. Research shows that engaging in flow activities can increase our happiness, creativity, and productivity.

- **Practicing mindfulness:** Mindfulness is the awareness of our present moment experience, without judgment or distraction. It helps us pay attention to what is happening in our body, mind, and environment. Research shows that practicing mindfulness can reduce stress, anxiety, and depression, and improve our happiness, health, and cognition.

These are just some examples of the many ways that the science of happiness can help us live happier and more meaningful lives. By learning about the research and applying it to our own situations, we can discover what works best for us and create our own happiness formula.

**How can we spread the knowledge and practice of happiness to more people and places?**

Happiness is a universal human aspiration, but how can we achieve it and share it with others? This is a question that has fascinated philosophers, psychologists, and policymakers for centuries. In this text, I will explore some of the latest findings from happiness research and suggest some ways to spread the knowledge and practice of happiness to more people and places.

According to the Journal of Happiness Studies, happiness research covers three main areas: theoretical conceptualizations of well-being, happiness and the good life; empirical investigation of well-being and happiness in different populations, contexts and cultures; and methodological advancements and development of new assessment instruments. Some of the key topics in this field include the role of positive emotions, meaning and purpose in life, character strengths, personal growth, resilience, optimism, hope, and self-determination in enhancing well-being and happiness.

One of the most influential studies on happiness is the Harvard Study of Adult Development, which has tracked the lives of 724 men for over 80 years. The main finding of this study is that the quality of our relationships is the most important factor for our happiness and health. Having close and supportive connections with family, friends, and community protects us from loneliness, depression, and physical ailments, and helps us cope with stress and adversity.

Another important aspect of happiness is how we perceive and respond to the world around us. Research shows that having an optimistic outlook can boost our immune system, lower our blood pressure, and increase our life expectancy. Optimism is not a fixed trait that we are born with, but a skill that we can learn and practice. One way

61

to cultivate optimism is to reframe negative events as temporary, specific, and external, rather than permanent, pervasive, and personal.

So how can we spread the knowledge and practice of happiness to more people and places? One possible way is to create educational programs that teach people the science and skills of happiness. For example, Harvard University offers a free online course called Managing Happiness that provides participants with data-backed strategies to make themselves happier. Another example is the Leadership and Happiness Laboratory at Harvard Business School that conducts research and creates resources for leaders to learn the science of happiness, apply it in their own lives, and share it with others.

Another possible way is to promote policies that support the well-being of individuals and communities. For instance, some countries have adopted measures of happiness or well-being as indicators of their progress and success, rather than relying solely on economic indicators such as GDP. These measures can help governments identify the needs and preferences of their citizens and allocate resources accordingly.

In conclusion, happiness is not only a desirable goal for ourselves, but also a valuable gift for others. By learning more about the science and practice of happiness, we can improve our own well-being and contribute to the well-being of others. Happiness is not a zero-sum game, but a positive-sum game that can create a virtuous cycle of mutual benefit.

**How can we make happiness science accessible, relevant, and engaging for diverse audiences and contexts?**

Happiness science is the study of what makes people happy and how to promote well-being in individuals and societies. It is a multidisciplinary field that draws from psychology, economics, sociology, neuroscience, and other disciplines. Happiness science has many practical applications, such as informing public policies, improving health outcomes, enhancing education, and fostering positive relationships. However, happiness science also faces some challenges in reaching and engaging diverse audiences and contexts. How can we make happiness science accessible, relevant, and engaging for everyone?

One possible way is to use storytelling as a tool to communicate happiness science. Stories are powerful ways to convey information, emotions, and values. They can capture people's attention, spark curiosity, and inspire action. Stories can also bridge cultural and linguistic gaps, as they appeal to universal human themes and

62

experiences. By telling stories that illustrate the findings and implications of happiness science, we can make it more relatable and memorable for different audiences.

Another possible way is to involve the audiences and contexts in the co-creation of happiness science. Rather than presenting happiness science as a fixed and authoritative body of knowledge, we can invite people to participate in the process of generating and applying happiness science. We can do this by conducting participatory research methods, such as surveys, interviews, focus groups, workshops, and experiments, that involve the stakeholders in defining the research questions, collecting and analyzing the data, and interpreting and disseminating the results. By doing this, we can make happiness science more responsive and relevant to the needs and interests of different audiences and contexts.

A third possible way is to use gamification as a strategy to enhance happiness science. Gamification is the use of game elements, such as points, badges, levels, feedback, and rewards, to motivate and engage people in non-game activities. Gamification can make happiness science more fun and interactive, as well as provide feedback and reinforcement for learning and behavior change. Gamification can also leverage social dynamics, such as competition, cooperation, and sharing, to foster a sense of community and belonging among different audiences and contexts. By using gamification, we can make happiness science more enjoyable and effective for everyone.

How can we overcome the barriers and challenges that prevent people from learning and applying happiness science?

Happiness science is the study of what makes people happy and how to apply it in their lives. It is based on research from various fields such as psychology, neuroscience, economics, and sociology. Happiness science can help people improve their well-being, health, relationships, and productivity. However, there are many barriers and challenges that prevent people from learning and applying happiness science. Some of these are:

- **Lack of awareness**: Many people are not aware of the existence or benefits of happiness science. They may have misconceptions or stereotypes about what happiness is or how to achieve it. They may also think that happiness is not a priority or a skill that can be learned.

- **Lack of access:** Many people do not have access to reliable and relevant sources of information or guidance on happiness science. They may face difficulties in finding, evaluating, or applying the evidence-based practices and principles of happiness science. They may also lack the support or feedback from others who are interested or experienced in happiness science.

- **Lack of motivation:** Many people do not have the motivation or willingness to learn and apply happiness science. They may have competing or conflicting goals, values, or beliefs that hinder their pursuit of happiness. They may also face challenges such as stress, anxiety, depression, or trauma that reduce their motivation or ability to change their habits or mindsets.

- **Lack of skills:** Many people do not have the skills or confidence to learn and apply happiness science. They may lack the self-awareness, self-regulation, or self-compassion that are essential for happiness. They may also lack the social skills, communication skills, or problem-solving skills that are needed for happiness.

To overcome these barriers and challenges, we can take some steps such as:

- **Raising awareness:** We can raise our own and others' awareness of happiness science by educating ourselves and sharing our knowledge with others. We can also challenge the myths and misconceptions about happiness and promote a positive and realistic view of happiness.

- **Increasing access:** We can increase our access to happiness science by seeking out and using credible and relevant sources of information or guidance on happiness science. We can also join or create communities or groups that support and encourage each other in learning and applying happiness science.

- **Enhancing motivation:** We can enhance our motivation to learn and apply happiness science by setting clear and meaningful goals, aligning our values and beliefs with our actions, and celebrating our progress and achievements. We can also seek help or support from others when we face difficulties or setbacks in our journey of happiness.

- **Developing skills:** We can develop our skills to learn and apply happiness science by practicing the evidence-based techniques and strategies of

64

happiness science regularly and consistently. We can also monitor and evaluate our outcomes and feedbacks and make adjustments as needed. We can also learn from others who are successful or experienced in happiness science.

## How can we evaluate the impact and effectiveness of happiness science promotion?

Happiness science is the study of the factors that contribute to human well-being and flourishing. It aims to provide evidence-based interventions and policies that can enhance the quality of life for individuals and societies. However, how can we evaluate the impact and effectiveness of happiness science promotion? How can we measure the outcomes and benefits of applying happiness science principles and practices in various domains and contexts?

One possible way to evaluate the impact and effectiveness of happiness science promotion is to use a mixed-methods approach that combines quantitative and qualitative data. Quantitative data can provide objective and standardized measures of well-being, such as life satisfaction, positive affect, meaning, and resilience. Qualitative data can provide rich and contextual insights into the subjective experiences and perceptions of well-being, such as happiness, joy, gratitude, and purpose. By triangulating both types of data, we can gain a more comprehensive and nuanced understanding of how happiness science promotion affects different aspects and dimensions of well-being.

Another possible way to evaluate the impact and effectiveness of happiness science promotion is to use a longitudinal design that tracks changes in well-being over time. Longitudinal design can capture the dynamic and complex nature of well-being, as well as the causal effects of happiness science promotion. By following the same participants over a period of time, we can examine how their well-being changes before, during, and after receiving happiness science interventions or exposure. We can also compare their well-being outcomes with those of a control group that does not receive happiness science promotion. This way, we can isolate the specific impact and effectiveness of happiness science promotion on well-being.

In conclusion, evaluating the impact and effectiveness of happiness science promotion is a challenging but important task. It requires a rigorous and holistic approach that incorporates multiple methods and measures of well-being. By doing so, we can generate reliable and valid evidence that can inform and improve the practice and policy of happiness science.

`

65

Happiness science is the study of what makes people and societies flourish and thrive. It draws on insights from various disciplines, such as psychology, neuroscience, economics, sociology, and philosophy. Happiness science can offer valuable guidance and tools for enhancing well-being and quality of life in various domains, such as education, health care, work, media, policy, and culture. In this text, we will discuss how to promote happiness science in these domains, and what are some of the best practices and principles for doing so.

One of the key principles for promoting happiness science is to use evidence-based methods. This means that the interventions and strategies that are implemented should be based on rigorous research and empirical data, not on intuition or anecdotal evidence. Evidence-based methods can help ensure that the interventions are effective, ethical, and appropriate for the context and the goals. For example, in education, evidence-based methods can help teachers and students learn about the science of happiness and apply it to their own lives and learning processes. In health care, evidence-based methods can help health professionals and patients use happiness science to prevent or treat mental and physical health problems, such as depression, anxiety, chronic pain, or cardiovascular diseases.

Another principle for promoting happiness science is to tailor it to the needs and preferences of the target audience. This means that the interventions and strategies should be customized and adapted to the specific characteristics, challenges, and opportunities of the people and groups that are involved. Tailoring can help increase the relevance, engagement, and impact of the interventions. For example, in work, tailoring can help employers and employees use happiness science to enhance their motivation, productivity, creativity, and satisfaction at work. In media, tailoring can help journalists and media outlets use happiness science to inform and inspire their audiences about the latest findings and applications of happiness science.

A third principle for promoting happiness science is to involve multiple stakeholders. This means that the interventions and strategies should not be imposed or delivered by a single actor or authority, but rather co-created and co-implemented by a diverse range of actors who have a stake or interest in the outcomes. Involving multiple stakeholders can help increase the legitimacy, ownership, and accountability of the interventions. For example, in policy, involving multiple stakeholders can help policymakers and citizens use happiness science to design and evaluate policies that promote well-being and social progress. In culture, involving multiple stakeholders can help artists and cultural workers use happiness science to create and disseminate cultural products that enrich people's lives.

A fourth principle for promoting happiness science is to foster collaboration and community. This means that the interventions and strategies should not be isolated or fragmented, but rather integrated and coordinated across different domains and levels. Fostering collaboration and community can help increase the synergy, learning, and innovation of the interventions. For example, in education, fostering collaboration and community can help schools and universities collaborate with other educational institutions, as well as with parents, families, local communities, NGOs, businesses, etc., to promote happiness science in education. In health care, fostering collaboration and community can help health care providers collaborate with other health care professionals, as well as with patients' families, friends, social networks, etc., to promote happiness science in health care.

A fifth principle for promoting happiness science is to ensure sustainability and scalability. This means that the interventions and policies that aim to enhance well-being should be designed in a way that they can be maintained over time and adapted to different contexts and populations. Sustainability and scalability are important for maximizing the impact and reach of happiness science, as well as for ensuring its ethical and social relevance. Some factors that can affect the sustainability and scalability of happiness science are:

- The availability and quality of resources, such as funding, staff, materials, and infrastructure, that are needed to implement and evaluate the interventions and policies.
- The alignment and integration of the interventions and policies with the existing systems, structures, and cultures of the target groups and organizations, such as schools, workplaces, communities, and governments.
- The engagement and participation of the stakeholders, such as beneficiaries, practitioners, policymakers, researchers, and media, in the co-creation, dissemination, and feedback of the interventions and policies.
- The monitoring and evaluation of the outcomes and impacts of the interventions and policies, using rigorous methods and indicators that capture both subjective and objective aspects of well-being.
- The communication and dissemination of the evidence and best practices of happiness science to the wider public, using accessible and appealing formats and channels.

By following these factors, happiness science can ensure that its efforts are sustainable and scalable, and that they can contribute to the long-term well-being of individuals, groups, and societies.

By promoting happiness science, we can help more people discover and cultivate their own happiness, as well as contribute to the happiness of others. We can also advance the field of happiness science itself, by generating more interest, support, feedback, and innovation. We can create a positive feedback loop between happiness science and society, where each enhances the other. We can make happiness science not only a scientific endeavor, but also a social movement.

# CHAPTER 18: The Future of Happiness Science

What does the future hold for happiness science? How will the field evolve and expand in the coming years and decades? What are the emerging trends and opportunities for happiness researchers and practitioners? What are the potential challenges and risks that happiness science may face in the future? These are some of the questions that this chapter will explore, based on the current state of knowledge and the possible scenarios for the future.

One of the main trends that will shape the future of happiness science is the increasing integration of different disciplines and perspectives. Happiness science is already an interdisciplinary field that draws from psychology, neuroscience, sociology, economics, philosophy, and other fields. However, as happiness science matures and develops, it will likely incorporate more insights and methods from other domains, such as genetics, epigenetics, artificial intelligence, machine learning, big data, biotechnology, nanotechnology, and quantum physics. These domains may offer new ways of measuring, understanding, enhancing, and manipulating happiness and well-being at various levels of analysis, from molecules to minds to societies.

Another trend that will influence the future of happiness science is the growing application of happiness science to various domains of life and society. Happiness science is not only a theoretical endeavor, but also a practical one that aims to improve the quality of life and well-being of individuals and groups. Happiness science can be applied to various domains, such as education, health, work, politics, culture, religion, and environment. For example, happiness science can inform the design of curricula, interventions, policies, institutions, products, services, and environments that promote happiness and well-being for students, patients,

69

workers, citizens, consumers, and inhabitants. Happiness science can also help evaluate the impact and effectiveness of these applications on happiness and well-being outcomes.

A third trend that will affect the future of happiness science is the increasing personalization of happiness science. Happiness science recognizes that happiness and well-being are not one-size-fits-all concepts, but rather depend on various factors that vary across individuals and contexts. Happiness science also acknowledges that individuals have different preferences, values, goals, strengths, weaknesses, needs, and desires that shape their happiness and well-being. Therefore, happiness science will likely move towards more personalized approaches that tailor happiness interventions and recommendations to the specific characteristics and circumstances of each individual. For example, happiness science may use genetic testing, brain imaging, personality assessment, or machine learning algorithms to identify the optimal happiness strategies for each person.

These are some of the possible trends that may shape the future of happiness science. However, there are also some potential challenges and risks that happiness science may encounter in the future. One challenge is the ethical dilemma of manipulating happiness and well-being. Happiness science may develop new ways of enhancing or altering happiness and well-being through pharmacological, technological, or genetic means. However, these means may raise ethical questions about the authenticity, autonomy, morality, and social implications of artificially induced or modified happiness and well-being. Another challenge is the social inequality of happiness and well-being. Happiness science may reveal or create disparities in happiness and well-being across different groups or regions based on factors such as income,
education, gender, race, culture, or geography. These disparities may pose social justice issues
and require policy interventions to reduce them. A third challenge is the uncertainty of happiness and well-being.

Happiness science may face limitations or errors in measuring, predicting, or explaining happiness and well-being, due to the complexity, dynamism, and subjectivity of these phenomena.

Happiness science may also encounter unexpected or unintended consequences of its applications or interventions on happiness and well-being.

These are some of the possible challenges and risks that may face happiness science in the future. However, these challenges and risks do not diminish the value or

70

potential of happiness science. Rather, they highlight the need for more research, innovation, collaboration, and dialogue among happiness scientists, practitioners, and stakeholders to address them.

Happiness science is a young, vibrant, and promising field that has made significant progress in understanding and enhancing human happiness and well-being. However, happiness science is also a dynamic, evolving, and expanding field that has many opportunities for further growth and development in the future. Happiness science is not only a reflection of the past and present, but also a vision for the future.

# CHAPTER 19: The Personalization of Happiness Science

In the previous chapters, we have explored the science of happiness from various perspectives, such as biology, psychology, sociology, ecology, spirituality, and more. We have learned about the factors that influence our happiness, the habits, practices, skills, and strategies that can enhance our happiness, and the challenges, paradoxes, myths, and measurements of happiness. We have also seen how the science of happiness can be applied to different domains of life, such as education, health, work, and society. And we have glimpsed into the future of happiness science, where new technologies and discoveries may offer new possibilities and opportunities for human flourishing.

But what does all this mean for you as an individual? How can you use the science of happiness to improve your own well-being and life satisfaction? How can you personalize the science of happiness to fit your unique needs, preferences, goals, and values? How can you create your own happiness plan based on the best available evidence and your own intuition?

The purpose of this chapter is to help you personalize the science of happiness for yourself. To do so, we will guide you through a series of steps that will help you assess your current level of happiness, identify your strengths and areas for improvement, set realistic and meaningful goals for your happiness journey, choose the most suitable interventions and activities for your situation, monitor your progress and outcomes, and adjust your plan as needed. By following these steps, you will be able to design and implement your own personalized happiness plan that will help you achieve greater well-being and fulfillment in life.

**Step 1: Assess Your Current Level of Happiness**

The first step in personalizing the science of happiness is to assess your current level of happiness. This will help you understand where you are starting from, what aspects of your life are already contributing to your happiness, and what aspects may need more attention or improvement. There are many ways to assess your happiness, such as using standardized questionnaires or scales (see Chapter 14), keeping a happiness journal or diary (see Chapter 8), or simply reflecting on how happy you feel on a regular basis.

One simple and effective way to assess your happiness is to use the PERMA model developed by Martin Seligman (2011), one of the founders of positive psychology. The PERMA model consists of five elements that are essential for human well-being: Positive emotions (P), Engagement (E), Relationships (R), Meaning (M), and Accomplishment (A). According to Seligman, these elements can be measured by asking yourself how often you experience them in your life. For example:

- **Positive emotions:** How often do you feel joy, gratitude, love, hope, curiosity, awe, or other positive emotions?
- **Engagement:** How often do you engage in activities that absorb your attention and make you lose track of time?
- **Relationships:** How often do you connect with others who care about you and support you?
- **Meaning:** How often do you find meaning and purpose in what you do?
- **Accomplishment:** How often do you achieve goals that matter to you?

You can rate each element on a scale from 1 (never) to 10 (always), or use any other scale that works for you. You can also add other elements that are important for your happiness, such as health, spirituality, creativity, or anything else that matters to you. The idea is to get a snapshot of your current level of happiness across different domains of life.

**Step 2: Identify Your Strengths and Areas for Improvement**

The next step in personalizing the science of happiness is to identify your strengths and areas for improvement based on your assessment. This will help you recognize what is already working well for you and what may need more attention or change. To do this, you can review your ratings for each element of the PERMA model (or any other model that you used) and ask yourself:

- What are my strengths? Which elements do I score high on? What am I doing right? What makes me happy?
- What are my areas for improvement? Which elements do I score low on? What am I doing wrong? What makes me unhappy?

You can also use other methods to identify your strengths and areas for improvement, such as asking for feedback from others who know you well (see Chapter 9), taking online tests or quizzes that measure different aspects of happiness (see Chapter 14), or simply brainstorming ideas based on your own experience and intuition.

The goal is to get a clear picture of your strengths and weaknesses as they relate to your happiness. This will help you focus on what matters most for your well-being and avoid wasting time or energy on things that don't make a difference.

**Step 3: Set Realistic and Meaningful Goals for Your Happiness Journey**

The third step in personalizing the science of happiness is to set realistic and meaningful goals for your happiness journey. This will help you define what you want to achieve, why you want to achieve it, and how you will measure your success. To do this, you can use the SMART criteria, which stands for Specific, Measurable, Achievable, Relevant, and Time-bound. For example:

- **Specific:** What exactly do you want to achieve? How will you know when you have achieved it? Be as clear and precise as possible.
- **Measurable:** How will you measure your progress and outcomes? What indicators or metrics will you use? Be as quantifiable and observable as possible.
- **Achievable:** Is your goal realistic and attainable? Do you have the resources and skills to achieve it? Be as honest and realistic as possible.
- **Relevant:** Is your goal relevant and meaningful to you? Does it align with your values and interests? Be as personal and authentic as possible.
- **Time-bound:** When do you want to achieve your goal? How long will it take? Be as specific and realistic as possible.

For example, a SMART goal for improving your positive emotions could be:

- **Specific:** I want to increase the frequency and intensity of my positive emotions by 20% in the next six months.

- **Measurable:** I will use a daily mood tracker app to record my positive emotions on a scale from 1 to 10 every day.
- **Achievable:** I have access to a smartphone and the app is free. I have enough time and motivation to use the app every day. I have some strategies and activities that can boost my positive emotions (see Chapter 8).
- **Relevant:** I value positive emotions because they make me feel good and enhance my well-being. I enjoy feeling joy, gratitude, love, hope, curiosity, awe, and other positive emotions.
- **Time-bound:** I will start using the app today and continue for six months. I will review my progress every week and adjust my strategies and activities as needed.

The idea is to set goals that are clear, measurable, realistic, meaningful, and time-bound. This will help you stay focused, motivated, and accountable for your happiness journey.

**Step 4: Choose the Most Suitable Interventions and Activities for Your Situation**

The fourth step in personalizing the science of happiness is to choose the most suitable interventions and activities for your situation. This will help you implement your goals and achieve your desired outcomes. To do this, you can use the evidence-based interventions and activities that we have discussed in the previous chapters (see Chapters 7 to 10), or any other interventions and activities that you find effective or enjoyable.

The key is to choose interventions and activities that match your strengths, areas for improvement, goals, preferences, personality, and context. For example:

- If you want to improve your positive emotions, you can choose interventions and activities that elicit or enhance positive emotions, such as expressing gratitude (see Chapter 8), savoring positive experiences (see Chapter 8), practicing kindness (see Chapter 9), or engaging in flow activities (see Chapter 9).

- If you want to improve your engagement, you can choose interventions and activities that increase your engagement in what you do, such as finding your strengths (see Chapter 9), setting challenging goals (see Chapter 10), cultivating curiosity (see Chapter 9), or learning new skills (see Chapter 10).

75

- If you want to improve your relationships, you can choose interventions and activities that strengthen your social connections, such as nurturing existing relationships (see Chapter 9), building new relationships (see Chapter 9), expressing appreciation (see Chapter 8), or providing support (see Chapter 9).

- If you want to improve your meaning, you can choose interventions and activities that enhance your sense of meaning and purpose in life, such as finding your values (see Chapter 10), discovering your passion (see Chapter 10), contributing to a cause (see Chapter 10), or creating a legacy (see Chapter 10).

- If you want to improve your accomplishment, you can choose interventions and activities that boost your achievement and success in life, such as planning ahead (see Chapter 10), managing your time (see Chapter 10), overcoming obstacles (see Chapter 11), or celebrating your achievements (see Chapter 8).

The idea is to choose interventions and activities that are relevant, effective, enjoyable, and feasible for you. This will help you optimize your happiness potential.

## Step 5: Monitor Your Progress and Outcomes

The fifth step in personalizing the science of happiness is to monitor your progress and outcomes. This means that you should keep track of how well you are implementing the strategies that you have chosen, and how they are affecting your well-being. Monitoring your progress can help you to identify what works best for you, and what might need to be adjusted or replaced. Monitoring your outcomes can help you to see the benefits of your efforts, and to celebrate your achievements.

There are different ways to monitor your progress and outcomes, depending on your preferences and goals. For example, you can use a journal, a spreadsheet, a calendar, or an app to record your activities, thoughts, feelings, and behaviors. You can also use scales, questionnaires, or tests to measure your levels of happiness, satisfaction, meaning, and other aspects of well-being. You can choose to monitor your progress and outcomes daily, weekly, monthly, or at any other interval that suits you. The important thing is to be consistent and honest with yourself.

Monitoring your progress and outcomes can help you to personalize the science of happiness in several ways. First, it can help you to stay motivated and committed to your goals, by providing feedback and reinforcement. Second, it can help you to

76

learn from your experiences, by revealing patterns and trends that can inform your decisions. Third, it can help you to optimize your strategies, by allowing you to compare and contrast different options and outcomes. Fourth, it can help you to appreciate your journey, by highlighting your growth and achievements.

# CHAPTER 20: The Reflection of Happiness Science

Happiness science is a field of study that explores the factors and outcomes of human well-being. It draws from various disciplines, such as psychology, sociology, economics, and neuroscience, to understand how people can measure, improve, and sustain their happiness. Let's examine some of the main topics and findings of happiness science, such as:

**The definition and measurement of happiness**

Happiness is a complex and multidimensional concept that can be defined and measured in different ways. Some researchers define happiness as a subjective evaluation of one's life as a whole, or life satisfaction. Others define happiness as the balance between positive and negative emotions, or affect. Yet others define happiness as a state of flourishing and fulfilling one's potential, or eudaimonia. Each of these definitions has its own advantages and disadvantages, and each requires different methods and scales for measuring happiness. For example, life satisfaction can be measured by asking people to rate their overall satisfaction with their life on a scale from 0 to 10. Affect can be measured by asking people to report how often they experience various emotions, such as joy, anger, sadness, and fear. Eudaimonia can be measured by asking people to rate their level of engagement, meaning, purpose, and growth in their life. These different measures of happiness can capture different aspects of well-being, but they can also vary depending on the context, culture, and personality of the respondents.

**The causes and consequences of happiness**

Happiness is influenced by a variety of personal and environmental factors that interact in complex ways. Some of the personal factors that affect happiness are genetics, personality, income, health, and values. For example, research has shown that about 50% of the variation in happiness is determined by genetic factors, such as the activity of certain neurotransmitters and hormones in the brain. Personality traits, such as extraversion, neuroticism, openness, agreeableness, and conscientiousness, also account for about 10% to 20% of the variation in happiness. Income can have a positive effect on happiness up to a certain point, but beyond that point it has diminishing returns. Health can also influence happiness both directly and indirectly, by affecting one's physical functioning and psychological well-being. Values can shape one's goals and expectations in life, and thus affect one's satisfaction and happiness. Some of the environmental factors that affect happiness are social support, culture, religion, freedom, and democracy. For example, research has shown that having strong and supportive relationships with family, friends, and community is one of the most important predictors of happiness. Culture can influence how people define and express happiness, as well as how they cope with stress and adversity. Religion can provide a source of meaning, hope, and belonging for some people, while freedom and democracy can enable people to pursue their own interests and preferences.

Happiness can also have various positive effects on other aspects of life, such as health, productivity, relationships, and social behavior. For example, research has shown that happy people tend to live longer, have stronger immune systems, be more creative, and perform better at work and school. Happy people also tend to be more altruistic, cooperative, and prosocial, and have more satisfying and stable relationships. These positive outcomes of happiness can create a virtuous cycle, whereby happiness leads to more success and well-being, which in turn leads to more happiness.

**The interventions and policies for enhancing happiness**

There are many evidence-based strategies that individuals and groups can use to increase their happiness levels. Some of these strategies are based on changing one's thoughts, emotions, and behaviors, while others are based on changing one's environment and circumstances. Some examples of individual interventions for boosting happiness are:

- **Gratitude:** expressing appreciation for what one has
- **Mindfulness:** paying attention to the present moment
- **Optimism:** expecting positive outcomes in the future

- **Kindness**: doing good deeds for others
- **Flow**: engaging in activities that match one's skills and challenge

Some examples of group interventions for boosting happiness are:

- **Social support**: seeking or providing help from others
- **Community involvement**: participating in civic or volunteer activities
- **Positive feedback**: giving or receiving praise or recognition
- **Teamwork**: collaborating with others towards a common goal
- **Diversity**: respecting and celebrating differences among people

Some examples of policies and initiatives that aim to enhance well-being at the societal level are:

- **Gross national happiness**: measuring the well-being of a nation based on multiple indicators besides economic growth
- **Well-being indexes**: ranking countries or cities based on their levels of well-being
- **Happiness audits**: evaluating the impact of policies or programs on well-being
- **Nudges**: designing choice architectures that encourage people to make decisions that benefit their well-being

## The challenges and opportunities for happiness science

Happiness science is a relatively new and rapidly growing field of study that faces many challenges and opportunities. Some of the challenges are:

- **The validity and reliability of happiness measures**: how to ensure that the methods and scales for measuring happiness are accurate, consistent, and comparable across different contexts, cultures, and populations
- **The cultural diversity and universality of happiness concepts**: how to account for the differences and similarities in how people define, experience, and express happiness across different cultures and societies
- **The trade-offs and conflicts between individual and collective well-being**: how to balance the interests and needs of individuals and groups, especially when they are in competition or contradiction with each other
- **The ethical dilemmas and responsibilities of influencing people's happiness**: how to respect people's autonomy and preferences, while also promoting their well-being and preventing harm

80

Some of the opportunities are:

- **The integration and collaboration of different disciplines:** how to combine the insights and methods of various fields, such as psychology, sociology, economics, and neuroscience, to create a more comprehensive and holistic understanding of happiness
- **The application and dissemination of happiness research:** how to translate the findings and implications of happiness science into practical and effective interventions and policies that can benefit individuals, groups, and societies
- **The innovation and experimentation of happiness science:** how to explore new questions and hypotheses, test new methods and measures, and discover new phenomena and mechanisms related to happiness

By exploring these topics in depth, we hope to provide a comprehensive and engaging overview of happiness science, and to inspire readers to reflect on their own happiness and well-being.

# CONCLUSION: The Science of Happiness

In this book, we have explored the science of happiness from various perspectives, such as biology, psychology, sociology, ecology, spirituality, and more. We have learned what happiness is, why it matters, how it works, and how we can cultivate it in our lives. We have also examined the habits, practices, skills, strategies, challenges, paradoxes, myths, and measurements of happiness. We have seen how happiness science can be applied to different domains, such as education, health, work, relationships, and society. We have also discussed how happiness science can be promoted and disseminated to the public and policymakers. Finally, we have suggested how happiness science can be personalized and customized to fit our individual needs and preferences.

The main message of this book is that happiness is not a fixed or static state, but a dynamic and flexible process. Happiness is not something that we have or don't have, but something that we do or don't do. Happiness is not a destination, but a journey. Happiness is not a gift, but a skill. Happiness is not a matter of luck, but a matter of choice. Happiness is not a one-size-fits-all solution, but a tailor-made adventure.

We hope that this book has inspired you to embark on your own happiness journey and to discover your own happiness formula. We hope that this book has equipped you with the knowledge and tools to enhance your positive emotions and well-being. We hope that this book has empowered you to become a happier person and to spread happiness to others. We hope that this book has contributed to the advancement of happiness science and the improvement of human happiness.

Thank you for reading this book and for joining us in this exciting and rewarding quest for happiness. We wish you all the best in your happiness journey and we hope to see you again in the future.

83